Ditch the Wheat
120 Paleo Recipes for a Gluten-Free Lifestyle

by CAROL LOVETT

VICTORY BELT PUBLISHING
LAS VEGAS

First Published in 2016 by Victory Belt Publishing Inc.

Copyright © 2016 Carol Lovett

ISBN-13: 978-1-628600-63-6

This book is for entertainment purposes. The publisher and author of this cookbook are not responsible in any manner whatsoever for any adverse effects arising directly or indirectly as a result of the information provided in this book.

Photography: Carol Lovett
Cover photo: Bill Staley and Hayley Mason
Design: Yordan Terziev and Boryana Yordanova

Printed in the U.S.A.
RRD 0116

TO MY GRANDMOTHER,
Irene Gerencser,
THE FIRST PERSON I KNEW
WHO EMBRACED LARD, GARDENING,
AND BAKING

Table of Contents

Foreword

Growing up, the bulk of my culinary instruction could be summed up by three skills: how to "bake" a potato in a microwave, make blueberry muffins from a box (which, as it turns out, contained more blueberry-colored food dye than actual blueberries), and test pasta "doneness" by throwing it against a wall.

Not exactly an impressive education, I know. It probably won't surprise you, then, that my first attempts at cooking real food from scratch were epic failures. My husband still teases me about my first experiment, in which I proudly presented him with a goat cheese pizza. His eyes bulged with the first bite, and he quickly reached for a glass of red wine to wash it down. I should probably mention that he hates red wine . . . he just hated that pizza more. (He did eat it, though. I love him for that!)

I wish I'd had this book back then.

Carol's recipes give back so many of the favorites that are often given up on a healing journey—bagels and bread, lasagna, chocolate cake, and more. They answer the question "What can I eat now?" with "Everything!" Yes, even if you're busy or inexperienced in the kitchen.

I chopped, sautéed, and baked my way through this book with three lively children whirling around me, moving my bowls and whisks and asking philosophical questions about Legos. Even so, each recipe came together beautifully.

That's not to say I didn't have moments of doubt. The first time I made her Ginger Beef Stir-Fry, I was sure that the recommended cooking time had a typo and the veggies were going to be overly crunchy. I followed the instructions anyway, and in return I was rewarded with a magical meal. In that way, Carol's recipes are a lot like her. Spend an afternoon chatting with her or baking her Chocolate Truffle Custard with Salted Cashew Crust—either way, you're likely to be reminded that things can come together in unexpected and wonderful ways, even when they don't seem to make sense at first.

The book you hold in your hands is an invitation to pleasure—in both cooking and eating. So many of the recipes you'll find in these pages are now staples in our home. I won't spoil the surprise by telling you which ones, because this is most definitely an adventure you need to take for yourself.

—Heather Dessinger, creator of the blog *Mommypotamus*

THE BIRTHRIGHT
OF ALL LIVING THINGS IS
HEALTH.
THIS LAW IS TRUE FOR
SOIL, PLANT, ANIMAL, AND MAN:
THE HEALTH OF THESE FOUR
IS ONE CONNECTED CHAIN.
ANY WEAKNESS OR DEFECT
IN THE HEALTH OF ANY
EARLIER LINK IN THE CHAIN
IS CARRIED ON TO THE NEXT
AND SUCCEEDING LINKS,
UNTIL IT REACHES
the last, namely, man.

—SIR ALBERT HOWARD,
FOUNDER OF THE ORGANIC FARMING MOVEMENT

Finding
PALEO

When my friends and I sit down and have conversations about our childhoods, only a few of us (including me) had health problems beyond ear infections. Now I can barely count how many of my friends' children have food sensitivities or allergies. The National Foundation for Celiac Awareness estimates that 18 million Americans have a gluten sensitivity. Unfortunately, the moment someone reaches out and questions whether she should remove gluten from her diet because she thinks she might have a sensitivity toward it, she is often met with pressure from her friends not to give in to the fad—not unless she has full-blown, diagnosed celiac disease. Many mothers are scolded over the idea of removing a core food group from their children's diet.

But I see the results of doing nothing: constant fatigue, bloating, gas, increased food sensitivities, mood issues, and so many more problems. I have also seen, in myself and many others, how the simple act of removing gluten from your diet can make all the difference, taking you from surviving to thriving. I wrote *Ditch the Wheat* to empower you on your gluten-free journey.

I take the Paleo approach to eating gluten-free because it takes into account the well-being of the animals you eat, the way the produce you purchase was farmed, and so much more that's important for health. I used Paleo guidelines (explained on pages 16 to 31) to create the delicious recipes in this book, which you can serve any night of the week to nourish your family. The recipes in this book are dairy-free (with the exception of butter in a few recipes), and many are nut-free. The food that you make should always be healing and delicious so that you can thrive. The recipes in this book will help you do that.

Do you know the power of food? Food can fuel your body, heal you, energize you, increase your fertility, and stabilize your mood. Food can also be a slow poison that causes you to feel tired, bloated, and gassy; to have mood issues; and to be in pain. How do your food choices affect you?

Make a stand to feed your body real food.

I'm Carol Lovett. I'm a food activist, cat walker, and beach-loving gal, and this is my story.

GROWING UP

I grew up in a middle-class family of six in southern Ontario, Canada. My father worked full-time, and my mother ran a day care out of our home. My mother believed in making food from scratch, which I always resented as a kid. Yes, I was that kid who refused to eat her mother's homemade chocolate chip cookies. My mom did most of the cooking and baking, and I have to admit that, though her baking was pretty good, her cooking was bland. It was my dad who was the chef in the family. He was the one taking weird concoctions and turning them into extraordinary main dishes.

At some point I became more like my father. At a young age, I began a love affair with food that is still going strong today. I enjoyed the processes of cooking and baking and became a natural at tweaking recipes and putting my own spin on classic dishes. I did have a few food aversions growing up that I still have to some degree. I refused to eat anything covered in gravy (still do), disliked pasta (until zucchini noodles came along), and could not and still cannot stand different foods touching each other on my plate.

I think I was around eleven years old when the first symptoms of irritable bowel syndrome (IBS) started. My family joked that the bathroom was my favorite place in the house. Since nature was calling ten times a day, it was easy to know where to find me. Along with IBS, I experienced bloating, daily headaches, anxiety, mild depression, and weight gain. I was a walking disaster as a preteen and all the way up to my twenties. It took me a long time to feel empowered enough to admit that I was an over-anxious and depressed young woman. I blamed myself for my moods and thought this must be who I was meant to be. No matter how much I tried to shake the anxiety and depression, I never could. Anxiety ruled every aspect of my life. I became a prisoner in my own mind. The only way I could get through social gatherings as an adult was with a glass of wine in one hand and food in the other.

The author, age two, and her older brother, Christopher, age four, making chocolate icing for a cake

DITCH THE WHEAT

The daily headaches affected my attention span in high school. I could barely focus on lectures, and the fatigue was debilitating. I eventually sought medical help, which led to MRIs and X-rays to rule out a brain tumor. With no answers from my doctor, my only solution was to continue taking ibuprofen daily. Little did I know that my continuous use of ibuprofen was contributing to a leaky gut (or "intestinal permeability" in medical terminology). At some point I embraced the chronic pain, and it became a part of me. I didn't know what it was like not to have a day with IBS, mood issues, and a throbbing headache. Fast-forward to college, and vertigo was added to my list of ailments.

The vertigo would come and go mysteriously. One minute I would be doing my homework, and the next minute the room would start spinning out of control. A vertigo episode is akin to that game where you place your head and hands on top of a baseball bat, with the other end of the bat touching the ground, run around in a circle, and then try to walk down a path. Random fainting followed the vertigo. I couldn't stand up without blacking out. I learned to stand up from my chair very slowly. I adapted.

HEARING THE MAGIC WORDS

In my early twenties I decided that I wanted to go back to university and earn a degree in business. The Great Recession had just hit when I resigned from my job. I was feeling good healthwise and my vertigo had settled down, becoming more of an occasional nuisance. I started my first semester, and then it hit me like a ton of bricks: my vertigo and IBS went haywire. I could hardly function. I endured these issues for a year, and then I finally built up the courage to say something to my family doctor. I was referred to a specialist for my vertigo.

For the first time I had a doctor with whom I felt I could share every complaint without feeling judged. I poured my heart out to him: "Along with feeling incredibly dizzy all the time, I have IBS, my stomach is bloated, I have headaches, and I feel tired. Can you fix me?" Then I asked the question that changed my life forever: "Do you think my bowel issues are caused by a gluten sensitivity?" He said, "Maybe. Try ditching the wheat and see how you feel." Those were the magic words that I needed to hear. It was Christmas 2010, and I went home and committed to a gluten-free diet.

I ditched the wheat 90 percent throughout the holidays and committed 100 percent to a gluten-free diet starting on January 1, 2011. After a short period of detox symptoms, I felt incredible. Brain fog, which I wasn't even aware that I had, disappeared. I woke up headache-free. Thirty pounds dropped off of me without much effort. I discovered that I had abs. My anxiety dissipated. My inner joy made a comeback. I felt free within my body and mind. I felt that I had become the person I was always meant to be.

MY TRANSITION TO PALEO

I had to learn a whole new language to eat gluten-free. I had an old copy of *Dr. Atkins' New Diet Revolution* to help me, and I identified myself as someone who ate gluten-free on the Atkins diet. My recipe searches online always led me to Atkins-friendly blogs, and these blogs taught me how to cook and bake with almond flour and coconut flour. A world of recipe choices opened up to me. One blog in particular made me want to start my own blog: Carolyn Ketchum's *All Day I Dream About Food*. Reading Carolyn's blog was like venturing into a forbidden world of food. Her site contained recipes for all the foods I had said good-bye to: cookies, breads, pizza, doughnuts. They were all there, made with gluten-free ingredients. The stories accompanying each of her posts made me feel like I was a part of her world. I wanted to emulate her.

I started my own blog in late December 2011, on my one-year anniversary of eating gluten-free, and I named it *Ditch the Wheat*. I was evangelical about spreading the benefits of a gluten-free, low-carb lifestyle, but I still had one issue: I have never been able to digest dairy well, and most Atkins-inspired dishes and snacks involve heavy cream or cheese, or both. Searching for gluten-free and dairy-free recipe inspiration on the Internet led me to Paleo blogs. Yet I resisted anything Paleo at the time because I thought it was a ridiculous-sounding diet. In fact, I thought it was the stupidest idea ever. Nonetheless, my blog quickly became a place to find gluten-free *and* dairy-free recipes. Eventually people started calling my blog "Paleo." Just as I had resisted the Paleo diet, I didn't embrace the new label people were giving my recipes.

The more I saw of these Paleo blogs, though, the more the Paleo approach to food began to rub off on me. I decided to move away from artificial sweeteners, and I bought my first jar of raw honey. It was a weird feeling for me—I had demonized carbohydrates and sugar for almost two years. I started to eat natural sugar and carbohydrates in moderation, and to my surprise I continued to lose weight. I also started eating sweet potato fries with my meals. Slowly my grocery store purchases started to include organic fruits and vegetables. A few months later, I proudly bought my first grass-fed steak. (Whereas the Atkins diet is meat-focused, Paleo stresses the consumption of *healthy* animal proteins that come from pastured livestock.) My blog started to reflect all these changes, and I officially started referring to my blog as a Paleo-focused blog.

Then in March 2014 I attended PrimalCon Vacation, a five-day event organized by Mark Sisson, an early proponent of the Primal lifestyle (which is very similar to Paleo), and heard a talk by John Durant, author of *The Paleo Manifesto*, who stepped up to the stage and shared a story about gorillas in captivity.

The gorillas lived in a safe environment meant to mimic the wild. They didn't have to forage for food or worry about being attacked. Their diets were overseen by staff, and they ate salad, fruit, and fiber bars that were supplemented with vitamins and minerals. Yet these gorillas were dying of heart disease, unlike their wild counterparts. The zoo gorillas had every advantage humans could give them for a healthy life, yet they were unhealthy.

Then the zoo staff did something radical. They changed the gorillas' diet to their natural diet—the diet meant for their species. Something magical began to happen. The gorillas lost weight, their behavior improved, and their risk of heart disease decreased. (For more about this study, read *The Paleo Manifesto*.)

This gorilla story shook me to my core. I had been the gorilla, eating foods that weren't meant for my species, and in many ways I still was.

Three months prior to that trip, I had signed a contract to write this cookbook. Honestly, I was lost on what kind of cookbook I wanted to write. I knew that I wanted to reach out to those who have felt lost, following diets that didn't work. After hearing the gorilla story, I felt a renewed desire to share with you a lifestyle that has captivated me, one revolving around real food that nourishes the body, with a few treats thrown in.

During the year that I worked on this book, its content took shape as some recipes were dropped and others added, and the latest changes embraced by the Paleo community were added just before going to press. Yet, throughout all these ebbs and flows, the main goal of *Ditch the Wheat* remained constant: to empower people who are sensitive or allergic to gluten and who are seeking practical recipes for a Paleo lifestyle. If you fall into either of these groups, you will benefit from the advice and guidance given throughout this book. The lucid breakdown of the Paleo diet, step-by-step cooking tutorials, on-the-go breakfast and lunch ideas, and 120 recipes, ranging from naturally fermented sauerkraut to meat bagels, sweet potato drop biscuits, pulled pork, caramel chocolate nut bars, and much, much more, are all meant to make your life easier as you transition to a healthier way of living and a new way of thinking about food.

Carol Lovett

About
THIS BOOK

In this book, I have tried to provide recipes that will help you transition to eating Paleo—and if you're already eating Paleo, you'll find a ton of delicious new recipes. These modern recipes are devoid of harmful processed ingredients that our ancestors did not eat, such as vegetable oils and fake butters. That said, my goal is not to copy the exact diet of a caveman, and I have used some healthy grain-free ingredients that for sure no caveman ate, like finely ground almond flour, to help you enjoy your Paleo lifestyle in a modern world. Most of these recipes do not require any special ingredients or equipment.

This cookbook will also introduce you to the story of our food and how it impacts our bodies. I'll show you what are considered healthy proteins, carbohydrates, and fats and share with you where gluten is hiding in your food, to empower you to successfully cope with your food sensitivity, even when eating out. I'll give you tips on how to stock your pantry and what kitchen tools you need. On top of all that, I'll provide you with practical guidance for making your life easier on the Paleo diet.

If you're not yet familiar with the principles of Paleo, I suggest that you read "The Why, What, and How of Paleo" on pages 18 to 24 and familiarize yourself with the ingredients and tools used to make Paleo-friendly meals before trying any of the recipes.

If you also want to avoid eggs, dairy, and nuts, you'll find a list of recipes that are free from these common allergens on pages 324 and 325, and icons mark these recipe pages for easy browsing:

egg-free   dairy-free   nut-free

Introduction:
THE WHY, WHAT, AND HOW OF PALEO

I love living in this day and age, but is it beneficial for our bodies? Processed foods, factory-farmed meat, and stressful lifestyles are changing our bodies, and not for the better. The Paleo diet is about nourishing your body with whole foods (with a few Paleo treats thrown in to help keep you sane). Let's take a quick look at what scientists have learned about the effects of diet and lifestyle on the human body over time.

WHY EAT PALEO

The Paleo diet is modeled after the diet of hunter-gatherers. Paleo enthusiasts believe that during the Paleolithic era, this group enjoyed the greatest health. It is important to note that there is no one definitive Paleo diet; there are many variations. This is borne out by modern-day hunter-gatherers: studies have shown that one tribe might thrive on a little meat and a lot of carbs while another eats a larger proportion of meat and fewer carbs, but they were all blessed with remarkable health.

In the 1930s, Dr. Weston A. Price wanted to find out why the majority of his dental patients had cavities, tooth decay, and facial changes resulting from crowded teeth. He especially wanted to know why his patients, living in the modern world, suffered while people living in desolate areas were free of these issues, even though they did not brush their teeth. He embarked on a journey across the world to study hunter-gatherers.

Dr. Price discovered that societies that stuck to their traditional diets flourished. They did not suffer from modern-day diseases. They had great fertility, and birth was easy for women. Their teeth were never crowded, and they had wide faces (a sign that the mother ate a nutrient-dense diet).

When Dr. Price researched communities that had adopted modern conveniences like white flour, sugar, and processed foods, he found that the generation born to parents consuming this diet did not have the same good health as their grandparents. The majority had cavities, their facial structures had changed, and their fertility was impacted.

An experiment by Dr. Francis Pottenger Jr. also shows how straying from a species' natural diet can affect future generations. The experiment studied over four generations of 900 cats, starting in 1932, and looked at how they did on their natural diet of raw meat compared to cooked meat. The first generation on cooked meat experienced degenerative diseases later in life, like many of our great-grandparents or grandparents have. The second generation experienced degenerative diseases in midlife. The third generation developed allergies, diseases, and fertility issues. The fourth generation suffered from everything the third generation did, plus 100 percent of them were infertile. This is why the Paleo diet focuses on the foods humans were designed to eat.

Wild animals IN CAPTIVITY AND **HUMANS** IN CIVILIZATION SHARE AN IMPORTANT QUALITY: WE ARE BOTH EXAMPLES OF SPECIES *living outside* THEIR **NATURAL HABITATS.**

JOHN DURANT,
*THE PALEO MANIFESTO:
ANCIENT WISDOM FOR LIFELONG HEALTH*

WHAT TO EAT

Here's an easy guide to what to eat on the Paleo diet. Bottom line: aim for real food. Visit your local farmers' market and shop the perimeter of the grocery store.

GOOD TO EAT	AVOID	GRAY-AREA FOODS
ORGANIC GRASS-FED BEEF	**GRAINS,** SUCH AS	ALCOHOL
ORGANIC GRASS-FED BISON	BARLEY	**NATURAL SWEETENERS,** SUCH AS
ORGANIC PASTURED PORK	CORN	COCONUT PALM SUGAR
GAME	QUINOA	MAPLE SYRUP
PASTURED POULTRY	RYE	RAW HONEY
CHICKEN	WHEAT	ORGANIC, GRASS-FED
DUCK	**LEGUMES,** SUCH AS	OR RAW DAIRY
GOOSE	BEANS	WHITE RICE
TURKEY	LENTILS	NUTS & SEEDS
WILD SUSTAINABLE SEAFOOD	PEANUTS	
(SEE PAGE 19)	**REFINED FATS** (SEE PAGE 23)	
FREE-RANGE EGGS	**PROCESSED FOODS**	
CHICKEN		
DUCK		
QUAIL		
ORGANIC FRUITS, SUCH AS		
APPLES		
POMEGRANATES		
RASPBERRIES		
STRAWBERRIES		
ORGANIC VEGETABLES, SUCH AS		
CARROTS		
PEPPERS		
ZUCCHINI		
ORGANIC STARCHES, SUCH AS		
POTATOES		
SQUASH		
SWEET POTATOES		
HEALTHY FATS (SEE PAGE 21)		

You'll find more on the "good to eat" foods on the following pages, and the "avoid" foods are discussed in more detail on pages 23 and 24.

The gray-area foods have been included in traditional diets for a long time, but experts are often divided about their place in a Paleo diet. I feel that these foods make life enjoyable when eaten in moderation.

Paleo experts used to recommend avoiding dairy. Then, as the movement progressed, dairy began to be seen as a food to include if you are not sensitive or allergic to it. Since dairy often doesn't agree with me, and to be extra cautious, I've excluded dairy from this cookbook with the exception of butter. (Ghee, though it's made from butter, is considered dairy-free because the milk proteins are removed.)

Natural sweeteners are used in limited quantities to add sweetness to some of the recipes in this book. Aim for a healthy relationship with sugar, one where you use it as an occasional treat.

White rice is the only grain that many Paleo enthusiasts consume. It is easy to digest, and when you cook it in bone broth instead of water, it is very nutritious. I have provided a recipe for Cauliflower Rice (page 272) as a substitute, but you can serve main dishes with white rice instead if you prefer.

MEAT

I never considered the lifestyle of the animals that provided my meat until I embraced Paleo. The way an animal lives is important not only ethically, because animals shouldn't suffer, but also because it impacts the nutritional value of the meat. Animals that are fed their natural diets and raised in environments that mimic what is natural for them are healthier and their meat is more nutrient-dense.

SEAFOOD

BEST BETS!

SALMON

SARDINES

MUSSELS

RAINBOW TROUT

ATLANTIC MACKEREL

GOOD CHOICES

OYSTERS

POLLOCK

HERRING

AVOID

KING MACKEREL

MARLIN

ORANGE ROUGHY

SHARK

SWORDFISH

TILEFISH

When I lived in Nashville, Tennessee, I often shopped at Whole Foods with my friend Caitlin. During one of those shopping trips, after I browsed the seafood aisle and selected a package of fish, Caitlin stopped me just as I was about to put my chosen fish in my cart. "You know there's a difference between wild and wild-caught, right?" I was like, "No . . . aren't they the same?"

Turns out, wild-caught fish start their lives in hatcheries and then are released into the wild to be caught. The Monterey Bay Aquarium's Seafood Watch program (www.seafoodwatch.org)—a great resource for sustainable seafood—warns that these fish compete with their wild counterparts for food.

That was the moment I threw up my hands and thought everything I knew about buying seafood was pointless.

Caitlin went on to say, "You can't just buy wild; you have to consider how it was caught in the wild!"

My head was about to explode. I just wanted to buy some fish, not feel guilty about how it impacted the ecosystem.

Bottom line: you are usually safe buying wild seafood, but if you want to buy sustainable seafood and seafood that is nutritious for you, it gets a little more complicated. You have to take into consideration where and how the fish was caught and weigh the pros and cons of farmed fish.

I rely on Seafood Watch, which categorizes seafood by best choices, good alternatives, and options to avoid. It specifies where the best seafood comes from and how it should be caught. Keep in mind, though, that it categorizes seafood based on how it impacts the environment, not on which are the most nutritious options for you.

Another good source of information about fish and seafood is the Environmental Working Group (www.ewg.org). It publishes a quick-reference chart that organizes fish and seafood by best bets, good choices, and options to avoid. The best bets are very high in omega-3s, low in mercury, and sustainable. Good choices have high levels of omega-3 and low levels of mercury but don't get points for sustainability. The fish to avoid have high levels of mercury, so they should not be eaten regularly. The lists at the top left are based on information from the EWG site, current as of 2015. Visit the site for the most up-to-date information.

ORGANIC FRUITS AND VEGETABLES

For me, eating organic is just about eating food that's as nature intended it to be, not genetically modified by scientists to withstand pesticides, then drowned in pesticides. The impact of pesticides on health is well documented—they're associated with everything from cancer to neurological problems to birth defects—and no one really knows the long-term effects of eating GMOs. (To learn more about the impact of food and environment on your immune system, read *The Paleo Approach* by Sarah Ballantyne.) Choosing organic produce not only gives you the most nutrient-dense, pesticide-free food for your body, it also supports the environment and helps preserve a green earth for yourself and for future generations.

Buying organic produce can be expensive, so to help you prioritize your purchases, check out the Clean Fifteen and Dirty Dozen lists at left, which are created and updated annually by the Environmental Working Group. The Dirty Dozen list identifies produce that tends to be heavier in pesticide content and is best to buy organic. When you're looking to save some money, the produce on the Clean Fifteen list tends to be safer to buy nonorganic.

GET TO KNOW YOUR FATS

Is fat nutritious and vital to your health? Absolutely, and I urge you to include it in your diet—but not just any fat. I remember the day I was told that butter was healthy. I was working at my first job out of college, and one of the supervisors was really into exercise and nutrition. One day we were chatting, and the topic of fat came up. He said something so appalling to me: "Butter is healthy, and you should eat it. Margarine is fake and will mess with your body." Say what?! It took me about four years to understand and agree with him.

Fat tends to get a bad rap, and it should, if it's a rancid, man-made fat like canola oil. Traditional fats that are found in nature, are sourced from animals raised on their natural diets, and are easy to render or extract, like lard, tallow, coconut oil, olive oil, and butter, nurture your body. You need fat to survive.

Did you know that your body uses fat to absorb fat-soluble vitamins? There's a reason vegetables and starch are traditionally slathered in fats such as butter. Dr. Steven Clinton of the Ohio State University Comprehensive Cancer Center performed a test in which participants were fed salad both without fat and with fat. The zero-fat salad included romaine lettuce, baby spinach, shredded carrots, and a fat-free dressing. After avocado (a natural fat) was added, the test subjects absorbed seven times the lutein and almost eighteen times the beta-carotene, both of which are linked to improved eye and heart health. Your grandparents didn't grow up eating steamed vegetables seasoned with only salt and pepper. Remember, natural fats have been around forever, whereas man-made, refined fats like canola oil have existed only since the 1970s.

☞ WORST-CASE SCENARIO:
YOU SPEND A MONTH
without
SOME FOODS YOU LIKE.

☞ BEST-CASE SCENARIO:
YOU DISCOVER
YOU ARE ABLE TO LIVE
healthier and better
THAN YOU EVER THOUGHT
POSSIBLE.

—ROBB WOLF,
THE PALEO SOLUTION: THE ORIGINAL HUMAN DIET

WHAT NOT TO EAT

REFINED FATS

Nutrition Facts	Amount/Serving	%DV*	Amount/Serving	%DV*
Serv Size 1 Tbsp (14g)	**Total Fat** 8g	**12%**	**Cholesterol** 0mg	**0%**
Servings: About 24	Sat Fat 2.5g	**13%**	**Sodium** 85mg	**4%**
Calories 80	Trans Fat 0g		**Total Carb** 0g	**0%**
Calories from Fat 80	Polyunsat Fat 3g		Sugars 0g	
	Monounsat Fat 2.5g		**Protein** 0g	
Percent Daily Values (DV) are based on a 2,000 calorie diet.	Vitamin A 15% — Vitamin D 15%			
	Vitamin B6 35% — Vitamin B12 20% — Vitamin E 15%			
	Not a significant source of dietary fiber, vitamin C, calcium, and iron			

INGREDIENTS: Natural oil blend (palm fruit, soybean, fish, canola, and olive oils), water, plant sterols; contains less than 2% of salt, sorbitan esters of fatty acids, monoglycerides of vegetable fatty acids, natural and artificial flavors, TBHQ (to preserve freshness), potassium sorbate, lactic acid, soy lecithin, vitamin B12, vitamin E acetate, vitamin B6, beta carotene (color), vitamin A palmitate, calcium disodium EDTA, vitamin D3

BAD FATS

- CANOLA OIL
- CORN OIL
- COTTONSEED OIL
- FLAX OIL
- GRAPESEED OIL
- MARGARINE
- PEANUT OIL
- SAFFLOWER OIL
- SESAME OIL
- SHORTENING
- SOYBEAN OIL
- SUNFLOWER OIL
- VEGETABLE OIL
- WALNUT OIL

Guess what this ingredient label is for? I'll give you a hint: I grew up eating it. It's an ingredient label for margarine. Note all the man-made fats, chemicals, and additives it contains.

In contrast, here's the ingredient list for grass-fed ghee:

100% *Organic* GRASS-FED BUTTER

Notice the simplicity of this list of ingredients. Here's a good rule of thumb: choose natural fats that your great-grandmother would have recognized and that have very short lists of ingredients, and avoid man-made fats with long lists of ingredients.

GRAINS & LEGUMES

There's a famous quote by Hippocrates: "All disease begins in the gut." That quote takes on new meaning when we look at grains and legumes and all the health problems that may be associated with them.

The problem with grains and legumes comes down to two kinds of compounds: gluten, a protein found in grains, and lectins, proteins found in both grains and legumes. These two compounds are dangerous because they can damage the lining of the small intestine, which can lead to a ton of health problems.

Here's how: The walls of the small intestine are lined with tightly packed cells that let nutrients into the bloodstream while keeping out all the bad stuff we don't want. Gluten and lectins can damage the junctions between those cells, and toxins, food particles, and bacteria can then slip through the holes. The immune system goes into action to destroy the bad guys, but that can lead to two other problems: (1) the immune system can start reacting every time certain foods are introduced to the body, leading to food sensitivities and allergies, and (2) in its efforts to fight the bad guys, the immune system can start to attack body tissues, leading to autoimmune diseases such as irritable bowel syndrome (IBS), Crohn's disease, ulcerative colitis, rheumatoid arthritis, Hashimoto's thyroiditis, or psoriasis.

The takeaway? Grains and legumes are no-nos if you want to keep your gut—and your body—healthy.

One legume in particular is problematic for other reasons: soy. Chemicals in soy mimic estrogens in the body, and that can cause hormonal problems. It's best to avoid all soy products, especially soybean oil, which is both soy-based and a refined oil (see page 23).

PROCESSED FOODS

I'm not against the idea of buying something premade. I personally prefer to buy condiments, coconut milk, and beef jerky rather than make my own. But I believe that you need to be smart about it and buy products that are beneficial to your body, not products that contain a ton of chemicals, food dyes, and other harmful ingredients. Look for items that are made with organic ingredients, and avoid foods that contain ingredients you can't pronounce—a sure sign that the food is highly processed.

The best way to avoid processed food is to make your food from scratch whenever possible. Try not rely on boxed cereals for breakfast or frozen meals for lunch at work—you'll find suggestions for quick and easy breakfasts and lunches on pages 50 to 53. Leftovers are also great for breakfast and lunch.

HOW TO MAINTAIN A PALEO LIFESTYLE

To me, calling something a "lifestyle" instead of a "diet" means that you don't feel the need to cheat; you love it. Have you noticed that when you begin a diet, you immediately start to crave the foods that are prohibited on that diet? I'd start hearing chocolate bars and cookies calling my name every time. It was like a battle going on in my head. Then the moment you cheat on your diet, you feel relief, followed by regret. Regret that you failed.

I'm not a fan of cheating. Lots of people follow Paleo "80/20"—that is, they eat healthy foods 80 percent of the time and whatever they want the other 20 percent. But I have a food sensitivity, and eating foods that my body reacts to is not nurturing. Is a bagel really worth bloating, brain fog, and IBS? Eating 80/20 is simply not practical for me and others who have debilitating problems with gluten. I suggest that you do this instead: re-create some of your favorite foods within the Paleo guidelines. The recipes in this book will help!

What does loving and maintaining a lifestyle that nurtures your body look and feel like? With Paleo, it's easy and practical. It doesn't involve counting calories, it doesn't involve hating yourself because you ate cake, and it doesn't involve going hungry all day because you don't feel satisfied after eating a "healthy" meal. The focus is on eating real food that makes you feel good.

To help you maintain your Paleo lifestyle, I've included a handy list of store-bought foods that often contain gluten (page 26), as well as tips on eating out (pages 28 to 30). On pages 50 to 53, you will find ideas for on-the-go breakfasts and lunches so you can eat healthy even when you feel rushed, and since cooking from scratch is such an important part of Paleo, you'll find cooking tips on pages 42 to 48.

HIDDEN SOURCES OF GLUTEN ON GROCERY STORE SHELVES

If you are sensitive or allergic to gluten, it's important to be aware of where it can hide in store-bought items that you may use to make the recipes from this cookbook, as well as other Paleo recipes.

Gluten is often hiding in these items:

- *Condiments:* mustard, some salad dressings
- *Sauces:* Worcestershire sauce, soy sauce, tamari. Flour is also used to thicken premade sauces.
- *Packaged broths*
- *Spice mixes:* Flour is sometimes used as an anticaking ingredient.
- *Processed meats:* cold cuts, pâté, pepperoni, sausages
- *Beer and malt beverages*
- *Anything containing barley or malt:* These are often used as sweeteners in chocolate, carob, and candy.
- *Bulk bins:* These can become cross-contaminated with grains.

Also beware of gluten-free baked goods. Wheat flour can become airborne and contaminate surfaces and utensils, even when they're used exclusively for gluten-free baked goods.

DON'T GET
OVERWHELMED
AND DON'T TRY TO CHANGE
EVERYTHING OVERNIGHT.
Take baby steps
AND CREATE NEW HABITS
AS YOU GO
SO THAT **YOUR HOME**
NOT ONLY BECOMES
a healthier one,
BUT A **HAPPIER ONE**
as well.

—KATIE, *Wellness Mama*

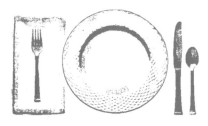

HIDDEN SOURCES OF GLUTEN AND SOY IN RESTAURANT FOOD

Since we don't live in a bubble, I want to help guide you through food choices you might need to make outside of your kitchen.

When eating out, I used to be slightly ashamed. I felt like I had to be prepared to walk into a restaurant, knowing exactly what I wanted, so I could avoid asking the question, "Is this gluten-free?" You know, the question that gets you strange looks and eye-rolls from waiters. I would go to the trouble of researching the restaurant's menu and calling the restaurant to verify questionable items, asking questions like, "Are your chicken wings lightly dusted with flour?" Then at the restaurant, I would order my gluten-free meal and ask for a side salad. I would receive my carefully researched and chosen gluten-free meal with a side salad that arrived containing croutons that were not mentioned on the menu. The horror! Embarrassed, I would pick off the croutons and just eat the salad.

I described my strategy to a fellow gluten-free friend. She said to me, "Would you feel the same way about a peanut allergy? Would you not fight for the same precautions if you or a loved one you were dining with had a peanut allergy?" For the first time, I realized that I needed to fight. If I didn't fight for my own well-being, no one else would.

Dr. Tom O'Bryan, who specializes in non-celiac gluten sensitivity and celiac disease, says that one gluten exposure creates six months of gluten antibodies. Just one exposure has the ability to cause inflammation for six months! I encourage you to take your food sensitivity or allergy seriously and stand up for yourself.

Many restaurants now offer gluten-free menus, but if you find yourself at a restaurant that doesn't, here's a list of foods and dishes in which gluten may be hiding. Always ask your waiter to verify that a dish is gluten-free. Also be aware of where other top allergens, such as soy, peanuts, and eggs, are likely to hide.

SALADS Ask if the salad comes with croutons or anything crispy or breadlike. Ask if your salad will be made in a clean bowl or one that may have been used earlier to make a salad with croutons in it. If the salad contains bacon bits, verify that they are real. Fake bacon bits are usually made from soy flour. Salad dressings usually contain soybean oil.

SOUP & CHILI Ask if the soup or chili is gluten-free. Often flour is used to thicken them.

SAUCES & GRAVIES Assume that any gravy or sauce is thickened with flour. Verify with the waiter and ask for your meal not to be served with the sauce or gravy. Sauces such as teriyaki contain soy, and cheap soy sauce often contains wheat. Also be aware that most barbecue sauces contain Worcestershire sauce, which is often not gluten-free.

CHICKEN WINGS Breaded chicken wings are obviously not gluten-free, but you'd be surprised at how many restaurants serve their non-breaded wings dusted with flour. Ask for your wings to be freshly prepared without flour. Be aware that they will likely be deep-fried in oil that is also used to deep-fry items containing gluten.

MEAT Ask how the meat is prepared. Is it marinated, dusted with flour, or cooked on the same surface as gluten-containing items? For example, breakfast items like fried eggs and pancakes are often cooked on the same surface.

EGG-BASED DISHES You might assume that you would be safe eating eggs, but scrambled eggs and omelets made at restaurants often contain pancake batter to make them fluffier. Yikes!

CRABMEAT It might feel silly, but you need to ask if the crabmeat is real. I have yet to be served sushi that contains real crab. Fake crab is made from Alaska pollock, and wheat is usually used in the manufacturing process to turn the fish into imitation crabmeat.

GARNISHES Ask how the chef garnishes the dish. I have been surprised to receive food with crispy onions sprinkled or sauces drizzled all over the top, none of which were described on the menu.

SWEET POTATO FRIES This is my favorite side dish to order. I always thought sweet potato fries were a safe option until I reacted a few times. I finally asked if the fries happened to contain more than sweet potatoes, and to my surprise I learned that many restaurants dust their sweet potato fries with flour to make them crispy.

BEER Beer is not naturally gluten-free, but some restaurants carry gluten-free beer. As an alternative, you can drink hard cider.

CROSS-CONTAMINATION Consider that chefs likely use the same surface to prep gluten-containing and gluten-free foods. The knife that sliced your grilled chicken might have sliced breaded chicken for another dish. The grill that cooked your bunless burger to perfection might have toasted someone else's hamburger bun. The oil that deep-fried your french fries was probably the same oil that deep-fried battered chicken wings. Ask for your food to be prepared in a clean area, cooked in new pans, and deep-fried in new oil. Be aware, though, that some restaurants might not comply with your requests.

I want to encourage you to be brave when it comes to taking care of yourself. I know that asking these questions in front of a date, your friends, or a group of work colleagues can be embarrassing. I've been in your shoes. But don't sacrifice your health to avoid a moment's embarrassment. In the long run, you will want to surround yourself with people who support you and don't find your health issues funny.

THE GOOD NEWS ABOUT EATING IN RESTAURANTS

Navigating a restaurant menu can be frustrating. I've probably made you feel like you will never be able to eat out again. But when I lived in the city, I ate out often and never felt restricted. It's all about knowing how to order for your food sensitivity or allergy. I want to empower you with knowledge and actionable steps to take. Here are a couple of examples of what I typically order:

·   A steak with a side of steamed vegetables and a salad

·   Chicken fajitas without the tortillas

Don't be afraid to walk into a restaurant armed with your own healthier condiments and seasonings. Many of my friends carry small containers of their favorite mineral-rich sea salt and ground pepper. Bring your own gluten-free soy sauce, coconut aminos, salad dressing, or gluten-free mustard. Make some grain-free tortillas (page 130) or buns (page 132) to take along. Do whatever you can to make eating out an enjoyable experience.

FIND YOUR WHY

Once you've decided to become that odd one out who declares to the world that you've ditched the wheat and so much more, I want you to consider your why. *Why* are you giving up so many food groups? Your why is going to drive you to success. It's going to be the key to maintaining your new Paleo lifestyle rather than allowing it to become last year's New Year's resolution.

Your why can and will evolve over time. My why used to be to stop the IBS, and then it became to prevent IBS plus lose weight. Now my why is to make my body the best it can be.

Terry Wahls is the inspiration behind my why. Even as I ditched the wheat and saw many benefits, I didn't truly understand the power of food. But when I watched Terry Wahls's TEDx talk, "Minding Your Mitochondria," I was stunned. Wahls showed me that it's within my power to nurture and heal my body through my food choices. I can't wait for you to discover your why and use it as a driving force for your health.

THINK OF
PALEO
as
a TEMPLATE,
NOT A RIGID
PRESCRIPTION.
THERE'S NO
one-size-fits-all
APPROACH.

—CHRIS KRESSER

Common
PALEO INGREDIENTS

The focus of this book is to bring you recipes made with natural and organic ingredients that cater to individuals on a grain-free diet. Eating grain-free and gluten-free is a central part of the Paleo diet. The recipes in this book were developed using ingredients that reflect the principles within these dietary movements: natural, organic, mostly dairy-free, grain-free, and low-inflammation.

ALMOND FLOUR AND ALMOND MEAL

You run to the grocery store looking for almond flour because you are desperate to enjoy cookies and bread again. In the health food aisle, you see almond meal. Scratching your head, you figure it must be the same. Ground almonds are ground almonds, right? What could possibly be the difference? While it's true that there is no difference in the ingredients, these two products will each result in a different baked good. Almond meal is coarser and usually made from almonds that have their skins, and it results in a lumpy, heavier end product. Almond flour is made from finely ground blanched, or skinless, almonds, so the results more closely resemble "regular" baked goods.

Almond meal is widely available, but where is the elusive almond flour? Don't worry, you can make almond flour at home by grinding blanched sliced almonds in your food processor until you get an extremely fine flour. You'll love the results. You can also purchase almond flour from Honeyville. This company produces the finest almond flour I am aware of.

Ideally, you should store almond flour in the fridge or freezer. The fat in the almonds can go rancid if you store it at room temperature long-term.

ARROWROOT STARCH OR FLOUR

Arrowroot starch and arrowroot flour are interchangeable terms for the same product. It comes from the arrowroot tuber and is white and fine, like regular wheat flour. I use it to add lightness to baked goods and to thicken sauces and jams. You can also use arrowroot starch in the same quantities you would cornstarch. I used Bob's Red Mill brand arrowroot starch exclusively when creating the recipes in this cookbook.

CANE SUGAR

This form of sugar, made from harvested sugarcane, is traditional, minimally processed, and not genetically modified. Regular white sugar used to come from cane sugar, but now about half of the sugar sold in the US is made from sugar beets that may be genetically modified. I use cane sugar in a few recipes to add sweetness when I don't want the flavor of maple syrup, honey, or coconut palm sugar.

COCONUT BUTTER Coconut butter is made from the meat of the coconut, and it is delicious. You can make it at home as you would almond butter: place coconut flakes in a food processor and process until smooth. However, for convenience, I prefer to purchase this item. You can heat coconut butter to a pourable consistency and use it as a glaze on baked goods. Store coconut butter in your pantry.

COCONUT FLOUR Coconut flour is my favorite flour to work with, yet so many people shudder at the thought of it. This is usually because they have had a bad experience using it and ended up with soggy, dense, and/or grainy products. But this finely ground flour made from dried coconut meat is not the enemy people think it is. When used in the proper ratios, it can produce the lightest and—dare I say—*fluffiest* cupcakes you will ever experience in your grain-free baking adventures.

Coconut flour has the highest fiber content of any flour. This is the key to understanding its finicky nature. When working with coconut flour, you must use more liquid than you normally would, and you must measure the liquids and coconut flour precisely. Store coconut flour in your pantry.

COCONUT MILK AND CREAM Coconut milk is made by mixing shredded coconut meat with water to produce a milk. It is naturally thick. In Paleo cooking, coconut cream is used as a replacement for heavy cream, and you'll see it in many of my recipes. Coconut cream is the cream that rises to the top when you refrigerate cans of full-fat coconut milk overnight. Look for organic coconut milk that is free of added ingredients, such as guar gum. I prefer the Aroy-D brand, which you can find in most grocery stores. One 13½-ounce can of full-fat coconut milk will give you about 1 cup of coconut cream.

COCONUT OIL Coconut oil is the fat derived from coconuts. It is a traditional fat in some parts of the world. I use it in place of butter in many of my recipes because many people—including me—who require gluten-free recipes also require them to be dairy-free. "Extra-virgin" and "virgin" on a coconut oil label mean the same thing. Look for "expeller-pressed" on the label, which means that the coconut oil was extracted from the coconut mechanically rather than with chemicals.

Coconut oil can be stored at room temperature; it remains solid at cooler temperatures but naturally liquefies in a warm environment. If you need solid coconut oil for a recipe, such as a baking recipe that involves creaming the fat, simply store your coconut oil in the refrigerator. Butter can replace coconut oil in any recipe in a 1:1 ratio.

COCONUT PALM SUGAR Coconut palm sugar is produced from the sap of cut flower buds from coconut palm trees. It tastes very similar to brown sugar, and you can use it to replace brown sugar in a 1:1 ratio. If you are unable to consume coconut palm sugar, simply substitute an equal amount of raw honey.

LEAVENING AGENTS Aside from mechanical leavening (such as whipping egg whites) and biological leavening (created by the activity of yeast), the most common way to give rise to baked goods is to use chemical leaveners, such as baking soda or baking powder. I use chemical leaveners in combination with some key baking techniques, such as creaming fats and sweeteners and sifting flours (see page 42), to create lift in my Paleo baked goods. I normally do not use store-bought baking powder because it often includes cornstarch as an anti-caking agent, a no-no on a grain-free diet. Instead, in my recipes you will see cream of tartar followed by baking soda. These two items team up to create a homemade baking powder.

LIQUID SMOKE Liquid smoke is made when water condenses and absorbs smoke. You can use it to add smokiness to any dish—a few drops will transform aioli or barbecue sauce into something magical—but remember, a few drops is all you need. You can find liquid smoke in most grocery stores.

MAPLE SYRUP I love this amazing natural sweetener, which is made by boiling the sap of maple trees into a syrup. You need to use real maple syrup, not the fake kind made from corn syrup. Dark maple syrup, previously classified as grade B, is the favored variety for cooking. It is amber in color. I use maple syrup when I want a distinct maple taste. In any of my recipes, you can substitute raw honey for maple syrup in a 1:1 ratio.

RAW HONEY Raw honey is unprocessed and unpasteurized. Many real-food experts believe that honey left in its raw state provides antioxidants, minerals, vitamins, and enzymes. Also, because of raw honey's 1:1 ratio of fructose to dextrose, it is easy to digest. Those who have a hard time digesting fructose can often tolerate honey. This sweetener is often allowed on diets for treating gut-related problems, such as the GAPS diet.

TAPIOCA FLOUR OR STARCH Tapioca flour and tapioca starch are interchangeable terms for the same product. Tapioca flour works just like arrowroot flour, except that it also adds a stretchiness to baked goods, so that a crusty loaf of bread has a little elasticity to it when torn apart. I used Bob's Red Mill brand tapioca flour exclusively when creating the recipes for this cookbook. Other brands can yield slightly different results, such as a darker crust, a denser texture, or a more watery batter.

YOU DON'T HAVE TO COOK FANCY OR COMPLICATED *masterpieces* — JUST GOOD FOOD FROM *fresh* INGREDIENTS.

—JULIA CHILD

Kitchen
TOOLS & EQUIPMENT

With the exception of things like English muffin rings and a spiral slicer, the tools and equipment that you will need to make the recipes in this book are very common. You probably already own most of them. If you don't have the exact sizes of pots and pans called for in a recipe, just use what you already own and reduce the size of the recipe or cook it in two batches.

KITCHEN TOOLS

BOX GRATER OR MICROPLANE EXTRA-COARSE GRATER

I use the large holes on a box grater to shred yuca for Yuca Hash Browns (page 158). An extra-coarse or coarse Microplane would also work for this purpose. I always wash this item in the dishwasher because food gets stuck to the grater and is hard to wash off without cutting yourself.

CUTTING BOARD

Cutting boards generally are made of wood or plastic. Keep in mind that wooden cutting boards need to be hand-washed, whereas plastic cutting boards can go in the dishwasher. Use cutting boards in a variety of sizes. I always reach for a small cutting board to chop an onion. I rely on my large cutting board when I need to cut up a whole chicken. When carving cooked meat, it is useful to use a large cutting board that has an indented edge, which will catch the juice of the meat instead of allowing it to flow all over your countertop.

ENGLISH MUFFIN RINGS

These stainless-steel rings usually come in a set of four that are 3¾ inches in diameter by 1 inch deep. I use them for baking Sandwich Buns (page 132). The rings hold the batter in place long enough to form the shape of a bun.

FLEXIBLE SILICONE SPATULA

Spatulas can be purchased individually or as a set. Sets usually include small, medium, and large spatulas. I find it handy to have a set with different sizes. Silicone spatulas can be used for cold and hot applications.

FOOD SCALE

A food scale is helpful for measuring baking ingredients and the cabbage used in Raw Sauerkraut (page 90). Look for one that has an easy-to-clean surface. I prefer a high-precision digital scale.

KITCHEN TIMER

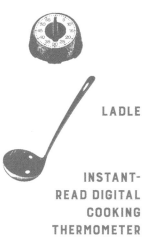

I use my cell phone or the timer function on my oven. If you do not have either of these, a kitchen timer comes in handy so you know when to take that succulent roast chicken out of the oven. It helps prevent you from burning Chocolate Chip Cookies (page 306). Pick a timer that you like and that is easy to use, with an alarm that is loud enough to hear from another room in your home.

LADLE

Ladles are great for scooping the contents of soups or stews into a bowl. They come in a variety of sizes, but I prefer a standard-sized soup ladle.

INSTANT-READ DIGITAL COOKING THERMOMETER

This type of thermometer can replace a candy thermometer, deep-frying thermometer, or a meat thermometer. I prefer the type that has a long cord that connects to a thermometer on one end and a small digital unit on the other end. You can program the thermometer to beep when the item has reached a certain temperature, you can easily switch between Celsius and Fahrenheit, and the readings are instant.

MANDOLINE SLICER WITH GUARD

A mandoline is an affordable alternative to a food processor for slicing. I usually use my mandoline to quickly slice pizza toppings. I want to emphasize the use of a guard with this tool. Guards are sold with the mandoline slicer and protect your hand from getting sliced. The next time you slice something thinly, make sure to remember safety first. You can choose different thicknesses by changing the setting.

3-PIECE MIXING BOWL SET

Stock your kitchen with a variety of mixing bowls in the following sizes: 1½-quart, 3-quart, and 5-quart. Each size will come in handy for baking or other kitchen tasks.

DRY MEASURING CUPS

Use these measuring cups for dry ingredients, such as almond flour. Measuring cups usually come in these sizes: ¼-cup, ⅓-cup, ½-cup, ⅔-cup, ¾-cup, and 1-cup. Pour the dry ingredient into the cup and then use the edge of a knife to sweep across the cup, removing the excess. Do not use the "scoop and level" method, which entails using the measuring cup to scoop flour directly out of the bag and then leveling it off. You will end up with a more heavily packed cup this way. I prefer measuring cups with handles to the pretty pottery type.

LIQUID MEASURING CUPS

This type of measuring cup should be clear for easy reading. To measure the amount of liquid, fill the cup to the desired quantity and bend down to view at eye level. The liquid should hit the measuring line perfectly. If not, add or remove liquid. This step is particularly important for recipes that use coconut flour because it is very sensitive to how much liquid is used.

MEASURING SPOONS

When purchasing measuring spoons, go for a complete set of six that typically includes the following: ⅛-teaspoon, ¼-teaspoon, ½-teaspoon, 1-teaspoon, 1-tablespoon, and ½-tablespoon or ¾-teaspoon sizes. Measuring spoons can be used for dry or wet ingredients. I recommend that you use ones with the measurements written clearly to avoid measuring the wrong quantity. When measuring, make sure to use something like the edge of a knife to gently sweep off the excess ingredient. Avoid using heaping spoonfuls of ingredients or less-than-full quantities (usually called "scant"), unless a recipe calls for it.

ROLLING PIN

Rolling pins come in wooden, plastic, or stone. I prefer stone or plastic because they are easier to clean than a wooden one. To clean any rolling pin, wipe it with a clean cloth. Using water repeatedly can damage a wooden rolling pin. I personally love the look and heaviness of my white marble rolling pin, which I bought a long time ago for five dollars at a flea market!

SIEVE

These stainless-steel mesh strainers come in small, medium, and large sizes. Depending on the manufacturer, the sizes range from approximately 3 to 4 inches, 5 to 7 inches, and 8 to 9 inches in diameter. I usually use a medium-sized sieve to sift coconut flour. You can use it to sift any dry ingredient. I also use this tool to strain pureed fruits to remove the seeds.

SLOTTED SPATULA

A slotted spatula is great for flipping pan-fried foods. I prefer stainless-steel over those with a nonstick surface.

SLOTTED SPOON

Use this spoon anytime you want to scoop out the food but leave the liquid—for example, when removing vegetables from boiling water.

SPIDER STRAINER (ALSO KNOWN AS A WOK STRAINER)

This tool is used to lift deep-fried foods out of the hot oil and allow the excess oil to drip off the food and back into the pot.

SPIRAL SLICER

Also known as a Spiralizer, the spiral slicer is a recent addition to most Paleo kitchens, but it's become so fundamental to Paleo cooking that it's hard to imagine making Paleo meals without one. I prefer the Paderno brand. It is made from plastic and has suction cups that adhere to the counter. It comes with a variety of blades for multiple noodle sizes. You can make noodles out of hard items, like celery root, or softer items, like zucchini.

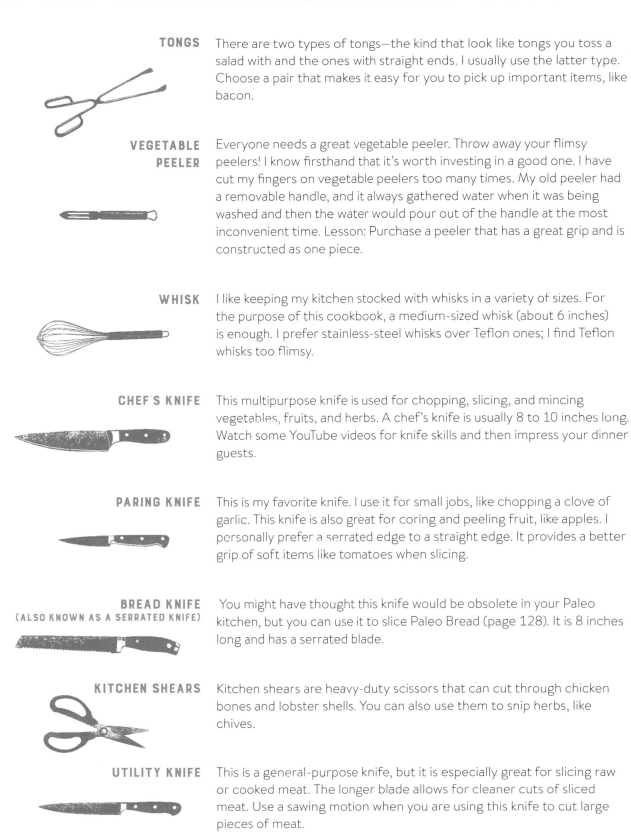

TONGS

There are two types of tongs—the kind that look like tongs you toss a salad with and the ones with straight ends. I usually use the latter type. Choose a pair that makes it easy for you to pick up important items, like bacon.

VEGETABLE PEELER

Everyone needs a great vegetable peeler. Throw away your flimsy peelers! I know firsthand that it's worth investing in a good one. I have cut my fingers on vegetable peelers too many times. My old peeler had a removable handle, and it always gathered water when it was being washed and then the water would pour out of the handle at the most inconvenient time. Lesson: Purchase a peeler that has a great grip and is constructed as one piece.

WHISK

I like keeping my kitchen stocked with whisks in a variety of sizes. For the purpose of this cookbook, a medium-sized whisk (about 6 inches) is enough. I prefer stainless-steel whisks over Teflon ones; I find Teflon whisks too flimsy.

CHEF'S KNIFE

This multipurpose knife is used for chopping, slicing, and mincing vegetables, fruits, and herbs. A chef's knife is usually 8 to 10 inches long. Watch some YouTube videos for knife skills and then impress your dinner guests.

PARING KNIFE

This is my favorite knife. I use it for small jobs, like chopping a clove of garlic. This knife is also great for coring and peeling fruit, like apples. I personally prefer a serrated edge to a straight edge. It provides a better grip of soft items like tomatoes when slicing.

BREAD KNIFE
(ALSO KNOWN AS A SERRATED KNIFE)

You might have thought this knife would be obsolete in your Paleo kitchen, but you can use it to slice Paleo Bread (page 128). It is 8 inches long and has a serrated blade.

KITCHEN SHEARS

Kitchen shears are heavy-duty scissors that can cut through chicken bones and lobster shells. You can also use them to snip herbs, like chives.

UTILITY KNIFE

This is a general-purpose knife, but it is especially great for slicing raw or cooked meat. The longer blade allows for cleaner cuts of sliced meat. Use a sawing motion when you are using this knife to cut large pieces of meat.

COOKWARE & BAKEWARE

CAST-IRON SKILLET

This pan is well suited for sautéing and searing because of its retention and even distribution of heat. To season your cast-iron skillet, coat it with coconut oil and place it on a rimmed baking sheet in a 300°F oven for an hour. To clean your skillet, sprinkle it with coarse salt and scrub with paper towels or a cloth. Be sure to avoid soaps and detergents. If your pan needs a deeper clean, you may use hot water and a scrub brush. Cast-iron skillets are not meant for cooking tomato-based sauces or other acidic foods. If you take good care of your cast-iron skillet, it will last you a lifetime.

DUTCH OVEN

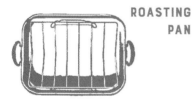

Use a 5- to 6-quart Dutch oven to make delicious braised meats and vegetables, as well as hearty stews. The Dutch oven retains and evenly distributes heat. Make sure that your Dutch oven has oven-safe handles and knobs so you can use it in the oven.

LARGE STOCKPOT

Be sure to have an 8- to 10-quart stockpot to make soup and stock. These pots also come in handy for steaming lobster!

ROASTING PAN

A generous-sized roasting pan is great for cooking roasts, poultry, fish, and vegetables. With the addition of a rack, this pan allows air to circulate around the meat or vegetables for even cooking. You can also collect drippings to make delicious sauces and gravies.

SAUCEPAN

This pan's straight, tall sides hold in moisture to steam and blanch vegetables. It is also well suited for making sauces and soups. Look for a thick-bottomed stainless-steel saucepan.

SAUTÉ PAN

This pan has straight sides, creating a large surface area on the bottom of the pan, which makes it ideal for cooking meats and reducing pan sauces. Just like saucepans, heavy-duty stainless-steel sauté pans are best.

COOKIE SHEET

Look for a cookie sheet with a small rim on one or two sides. This makes it easy to grab hold of the hot cookie sheet when removing it from the oven or sliding cookies onto a wire rack.

RIMMED BAKING SHEET

This shallow, heavy-duty aluminum baking pan with 1-inch sides is great for roasting vegetables. I prefer baking sheets that are 18 by 13 by 1 inch.

MUFFIN TIN

This is a must for any baker to make muffins and cupcakes. I always use a standard 12-cup pan.

LOAF PAN

Glass and metal loaf pans work well for baking bread and cooking meatloaf. For easy removal of food, line the pan with parchment paper, leaving a 2-inch overhang on each side. I use an 8½-by-4½-inch loaf pan.

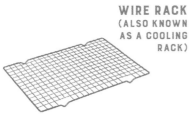

WIRE RACK (ALSO KNOWN AS A COOLING RACK)

A raised wire rack allows baked goods to fully cool before storing or adding icing or glaze. Choose a stainless-steel version with feet on the bottom. When transferring delicate items like cookies straight out of the oven to a wire rack, leave them on the sheet for about 5 minutes and then transfer. This will allow them to become firmer, so they're less likely to break when you transfer them.

MISCELLANEOUS EQUIPMENT

SLOW COOKER

This is a must-have small kitchen appliance, perfect for weeknight meals in busy households. The low cooking temperature allows foods to simmer for long periods of time, making it ideal for pot roasts, stews, and soups. Slow cooking is actually a traditional form of cooking. The slow cooker recipes in this book require a 6-quart or larger slow cooker.

HAND BLENDER

Also known as an immersion blender or stick blender, this handy, compact tool allows you to puree foods right in the cooking pot. It is great for making homemade aioli. I use my hand blender for almost everything I would use a food processor for, except chopping. Always pulse a few times, let the machine rest, and then pulse again, because the motor does overheat quickly.

FOOD PROCESSOR

Food processors work perfectly to smoothly blend or chop ingredients. You can purchase them in large or small sizes, but aim for the larger size since it will work better for many recipes. Purchase a good brand, such as Hamilton Beach or Cuisinart, because you will use this tool often in your cooking adventures.

Tips &
TRICKS

In this section, I share some basic cooking and baking tips and tricks with you that will ease your transition to baking gluten-free and cooking meals from scratch, including how to make Paleo classics that may be new to you, like spiral-cut vegetable noodles. I'll also share some quick breakfast and lunch ideas to help you maintain a Paleo lifestyle, even when you're in a time crunch.

HOW TO BAKE WITH SUCCESS

Since Paleo baked goods are made with flours that do not have gluten, they tend not to rise in the same manner as baked goods made with flours that do have gluten, such as wheat flour. I've found that the use of a chemical leavener and the following key baking techniques help greatly in mimicking the loft and texture you get in conventional baked items.

SIFT COCONUT FLOUR

When coconut flour is used in a recipe, always take the time to sift the flour. Coconut flour is naturally lumpy, and you don't want to bite into your coconut flour cake and find a chunk of flour. Sifting adds a few seconds of additional work but I highly recommend it.

WHIP EGG WHITES

You will notice I recommend whipping the egg whites in the majority of the coconut flour recipes. By taking the time to do a little more than simply mix the wet ingredients with the dry ingredients, you will get a much better texture. To whip egg whites, place them in a clean stainless-steel bowl and, using a stand mixer with the whisk attachment or a hand mixer, whip the egg whites on high speed until they look like meringue. Stop at that point; overmixing can ruin your egg whites.

CREAM FATS AND SWEETENERS

I recommend creaming coconut oil (or your preferred baking fat) and the sweetener because it helps create air pockets in the baked goods, creating a light, fluffy texture. It takes 5 to 10 minutes to properly cream the fat and sweetener together. You'll know you are done creaming when the mixture starts to form ridges and starts sticking to the sides of the bowl. I always cream with a stand mixer or hand mixer.

USE EGGS AT ROOM TEMPERATURE

I recommend bringing eggs to room temperature before using them. It is not necessary, but eggs at room temperature expand better. The more warmth you apply to eggs, the more they expand.

HOW TO CUT UP A WHOLE CHICKEN

I used to exclusively buy chicken breasts. When I switched to better-quality chicken, it was too expensive for my budget! To save money, I started purchasing whole chickens and cutting them up myself. Also, many farms will not sell you individual chicken pieces, so it's worth knowing how to cut up a whole chicken.

Cutting up a chicken is actually very easy. To discover where to cut the legs, thighs, and wings, you simply wiggle it to find the joint. Take a large, sharp knife and cut through the joint. Cutting the breast uses another technique, explained below.

Start by laying the chicken on its back. Place your hand on one of the wings and wiggle to determine where the joint attaches to the breast. Use a sharp knife to cut through the ball joint where it meets the breast. Repeat with the other wing. (See figure 1.)

Next, place your hand on one of the legs and pull the leg away from the body to see where the thigh attaches to the breast. Remove the whole leg (drumstick and thigh) by cutting through the skin between the thigh and the breast. Repeat with the other leg. (See figures 2 and 3.)

If you want to detach the thighs from the drumsticks, place each leg skin side down. Wiggle to see where the ball joint between the drumstick and thigh is located. Cut through the joint area. Repeat with the other leg. (See figure 4.)

After you remove the wings, legs, and thighs, you will be left with the two breasts.

Turn the chicken over, so the back is facing up. Locate the spine of the chicken. Start at one end of the spine and feel for the rib cage. Take your knife or poultry shears and gently cut between the rib cage and the breast. Do that for each breast. (See figure 5.) You should be able to remove the two breasts from the spine and rib cage. Save the bones for chicken broth. I add the bones to a bag in the freezer until I am ready to make broth.

Take your knife and cut the breasts into two halves. (See figures 6 and 7.)

Note: *Key point: Always wiggle, then cut! Wiggle again, then cut again! It may sound funny, but it makes a difference.*

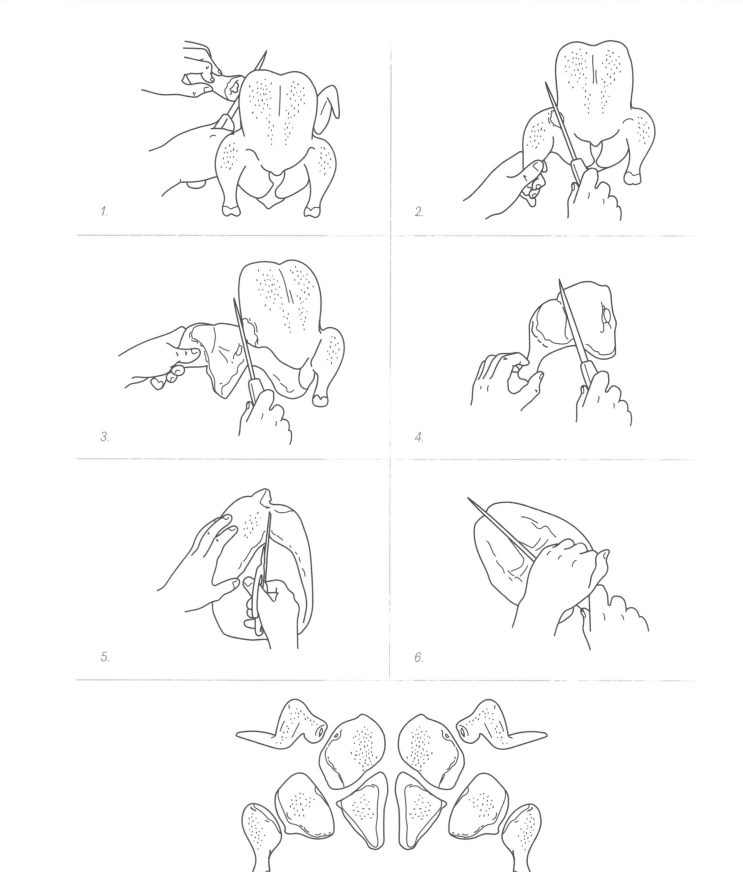

1.

2.

3.

4.

5.

6.

7.

HOW TO COOK VEGGIES AND STARCHES

Cooking is a lost art. Here's a little secret: I didn't know the first thing about cooking until I started making food from scratch to improve my health and control what I was putting into my body. If you're new to cooking, too, here are some basic—but delicious—methods for cooking veggies and starches.

GENERAL FIRST STEP Wash, dry, peel, and chop the vegetables or starches you want to cook.

SAUTÉ Pick a skillet that is the appropriate size. Place 2 tablespoons of olive oil or your preferred fat in it and turn the heat to medium-high. Heat up the skillet and fat, then add the vegetables or starches. Sprinkle salt and pepper on them and any other desired herbs and spices. You can place a lid on the skillet to gently steam them and cook them faster. Stir often, and if the veggies are sticking to the pan, add more oil. Remove from heat after 2 to 10 minutes. They're done when they are fork-tender (meaning a fork can easily pierce it). Some vegetables, like zucchini, cook fast, but others, like dense root vegetables, take longer. The size of the dice, chop, or slice also affects cooking time.

STEAM Fill an appropriate-sized pot with at least 2 inches of water. Place a vegetable steamer in the pot. Add the vegetables or starches to the steamer and place the lid on top. Turn the heat to high and steam for 10 minutes, or until fork-tender. Transfer to a bowl, add at least 1 tablespoon of fat, such as ghee, and season with salt. Toss to coat and serve immediately.

ROAST Preheat the oven to 400°F. This temperature is a general guideline and works well with most vegetables and starches. Make sure you cut up all the vegetables into similar sizes. Place all of them in a roasting pan and drizzle with enough fat to coat them all. Sprinkle with salt and pepper and toss. For added flavor, you can toss in garlic cloves, fresh or dried herbs, or quartered onions. Bake for at least 20 minutes to an hour, depending on the vegetable and size of cut pieces. For example, carrots generally take about 20 minutes. Starches such as whole potatoes, however, take at least an hour. When they are done, they will be fork-tender and should be crispy on the outside.

HOW TO MAKE PALEO NOODLES

People are always telling me they could never eat gluten-free or Paleo because they have to be able to eat pasta. These veggie noodle ideas are a great replacement for grain-based pasta and have converted a ton of people. As another plus, they're an easy way to get your kids to eat more veggies.

CABBAGE

Use a mandoline to finely slice cabbage, enough to replace the noodles in the recipes you are following. Heat 2 tablespoons of olive oil in a skillet on medium-high heat. Place the cabbage in the heated skillet. Sauté until soft, about 10 minutes. Add to your dish and serve.

CELERY ROOT (CELERIAC)

If you have never eaten celery root, it tastes like a cross between celery and potato. Peel the celery root, then use a spiral slicer to make noodles, following the directions that came with your spiral slicer. Boil the noodles for 2 to 3 minutes, until tender, then drain. Add to your dish and serve. Expect to use half of a celery root per person.

KELP NOODLES

Kelp noodles are rather bland. They do not have a seafood taste at all. Remove the kelp noodles from their package and add them directly to the sauce to warm, and then serve when ready.

SPAGHETTI SQUASH

Preheat the oven to 350°F. Line a rimmed baking sheet with parchment paper. Cut the squash in half lengthwise. This can be tricky, so take your time. Place the squash cut side down on the prepared baking sheet and bake for 30 minutes. The squash is done when a knife can be inserted through the skin. Let the squash cool until you can comfortably handle it. Use a spoon to scoop out the seeds and discard them. Then scoop out the stringy squash flesh, or "noodles," and use as desired. One medium spaghetti squash serves two people.

SWEET POTATO

Peel the sweet potato, then use a spiral slicer to make noodles, following the directions that came with your spiral slicer. Boil the noodles for 2 to 3 minutes, until tender, then drain. Add to your dish and serve. Count on one-half medium sweet potato per serving.

ZUCCHINI

Peel or leave unpeeled, then use a spiral slicer to make noodles, following the directions that came with your spiral slicer. Place raw noodles on a dish and sprinkle generously with salt. Leave for at least 5 minutes to draw out as much moisture as possible. Rinse the noodles, then blot with a paper towel. Heat 2 tablespoons of olive oil in a skillet over medium heat. Add the noodles to the hot skillet and sauté until tender, about 2 minutes. Add to the dish and serve. One medium-sized zucchini will make enough noodles to serve one person.

QUICK BREAKFAST IDEAS

You're rushing out the door and need something fast for breakfast. In your pre-Paleo mornings, you would have reached for the box of cereal or a breakfast bar, which are no longer options. Don't eat a breakfast consisting solely of a Paleo muffin or coconut milk yogurt—you'll be hungry again soon after. Eat a more balanced breakfast using one of the ideas below, which will keep you satisfied until lunchtime.

Leftovers. Think outside the breakfast box. Repurpose your dinner leftovers from last night as your breakfast.

Frozen sausage patties. Prepare a week's worth or more of uncooked sausage patties in advance and freeze them. To freeze them, place the patties on a rimmed baking sheet lined with parchment paper. Place the tray in the freezer and freeze until firm, about an hour. Once firm, place all the sausage patties into a storage container. Take a few out the night before and place them in the fridge to thaw (if you cook them frozen, they will take a long time to cook). In the morning, cook according to the recipe's directions. (See pages 140 to 143 for recipes.)

Bacon. Batch-cook bacon in advance; it's great cold or reheated.

On-the-Go Eggs. Batch-cook On-the-Go Eggs (page 150) in advance. They're delicious cold.

Fried eggs. These take just minutes to cook.

Hard-boiled eggs. Make a week's worth of hard-boiled eggs in advance so you can grab them and go.

Serve all of the above with Raw Sauerkraut (page 90) to aid in digestion, and add a quick vegetable, such as sautéed spinach or cucumber slices, to your breakfast plate.

ONCE YOU HAVE *mastered* A TECHNIQUE, YOU BARELY HAVE TO LOOK AT A RECIPE *again.*

-JULIA CHILD,
JULIA'S KITCHEN WISDOM: ESSENTIAL TECHNIQUES AND
RECIPES FROM A LIFETIME OF COOKING

QUICK LUNCH IDEAS

I get asked all the time, what are quick lunch ideas for workdays? The easiest solution is to make extra for supper the night before so you have leftovers for lunch. Another make-ahead idea is to batch-cook something you like and assemble your lunches all in one session on the weekend.

But let's face it, when it comes to lunch, everyone wants a sandwich or a wrap. In fact, when I first transitioned to Paleo, I didn't know how to eat lunch because I used to wrap everything in whole-wheat wraps. I thought it was a clever way to eat lunch on the go. But as I discovered, you can still enjoy sandwiches and wraps on the Paleo diet; you just need to get a little creative.

THAT'S A WRAP, OR SANDWICH

To make a wrap, use either my Grain-Free Tortillas (page 130) or try one of these wrap ideas.

VEGGIE WRAP IDEAS

Butter lettuce

Romaine lettuce

Iceberg lettuce

Aim for lettuce that is soft, not bitter, and flexible. Flexibility is key because it needs to be molded into a wrap without breaking.

MEATY WRAP IDEAS

Any cold cuts, such as roasted chicken, turkey, or beef

Bacon: Weave uncooked slices of bacon to make a wrap the size of a piece of bread, then either pan-fry or bake it.

BUN IDEAS

Two roasted, thick, oval-cut sweet potato slices

Two roasted portobello mushrooms (see Note)

Two large bell pepper slices

The Original DTW Meat Bagel (page 144)

Sandwich Buns (page 132)

Note: After roasting the portobello mushroom, squeeze out all the liquid before you use it as a bun. If you don't squeeze the mushrooms, the juices will be flowing all over the place as you eat your sandwich.

THREE BUTTER LETTUCE WRAPS

Here are three ideas for using butter lettuce as a wrap. If you're packing these for your lunch, wrap tightly with plastic wrap or reusable fabric wraps.

CHICKEN BLT — Butter lettuce, 2 slices cooked bacon, 2 thin slices tomato, either cooked chicken breast cut into strips or roast chicken from the deli counter, Homemade Aioli (page 64)

THE ITALIAN — Butter lettuce, 1 slice salami, 1 slice ham, 1 slice turkey, pickled hot peppers, 2 thin slices tomato, Homemade Aioli (page 64)

TURKEY PESTO — Butter lettuce, 3 slices turkey, 2 slices cooked bacon, 2 thin slices tomato, 2 tablespoons dairy-free pesto

Note: Here's a quick recipe for dairy-free pesto: In a food processor, combine ¼ cup pine nuts, ¼ cup chopped fresh parsley, 1 clove garlic, 1 teaspoon fresh lemon juice, 1 tablespoon extra-virgin olive oil, and sea salt to taste. Pulse until a paste forms. Keep stored in the fridge for up to a week.

GHEE

Yield: 1½ cups   *Prep time:* 5 minutes   *Cook time:* 15 minutes

I was introduced to ghee in university when I shared a house with fourteen guys and one girl. Seriously, fourteen guys! About a third of the guys were international students from India and Pakistan. Ghee was their staple cooking fat, and they would pull out huge containers of the stuff and start cooking omelets. At the time, I couldn't wrap my mind around not using butter. Now ghee is a staple in my kitchen, and I prefer to use it for sautéing and roasting. Ghee is butter for people who can't tolerate dairy; the process of making ghee removes the milk solids. As with coconut oil, you can store ghee at room temperature.

---

1 pound (2 cups/4 sticks) unsalted butter, cubed

1. Melt the butter in a 3-quart saucepan over medium-low heat. Once melted, the butter should separate into three layers: foam, golden, and solids. This should take only a few minutes.

2. Heat for 15 minutes. Turn off the heat, skim off the foam layer, and discard.

3. Pour the golden middle layer through cheesecloth into a large glass jar, leaving the milk solids at the bottom of the pan. Discard the milk solids. Store the ghee at room temperature.

Dairy-Free
CREAMY CAESAR DRESSING

Yield: About 1 cup   *Prep time:* 5 minutes

Because I had heard rumors that it contains anchovies and egg yolks, it took me years to try Caesar dressing. I just don't like anchovies; trust me, I've tried to love them, but it's just not going to happen. But I do like the anchovy paste in this recipe, and it's a must-have ingredient here. It gives you umami, and you want umami. Umami is that unique taste you get when you love something but you can't quite put your finger on what it is. Bacon is another source of umami, in case you wanted more reasons to add it to your recipes.

4 large egg yolks

1 tablespoon Dijon mustard

1 cup extra-light olive oil

1 tablespoon anchovy paste

¼ cup fresh lemon juice

⅛ teaspoon ground black pepper

1. Place the egg yolks and mustard in the bowl of a stand mixer fitted with the whisk attachment.

2. Turn the mixer to the highest speed and slowly drizzle in the olive oil, one drop at a time. Allow the olive oil to be fully mixed into the egg yolk mixture before adding more. Continue until all the olive oil is emulsified.

3. Add the anchovy paste, lemon juice, and pepper and mix until combined.

4. Store the dressing in the fridge for up to 1 week.

Maple Balsamic
SALAD DRESSING

Yield: ½ cup   *Prep time:* 2 minutes

This dressing is as dreamy as it sounds, and it pairs perfectly with any salad containing bacon. You can enjoy this dressing warm or cold. I find that it goes well with most forms of lettuce, but I like it best with spinach or mixed greens.

⅓ cup extra-light olive oil

2 tablespoons maple syrup

2 tablespoons balsamic vinegar

2 teaspoons Dijon mustard

½ teaspoon fine sea salt

1. Place all the ingredients in a bowl and whisk together until combined.

2. Store the dressing in the fridge for up to 3 weeks.

3. On the day you plan on using the dressing, check to see if the olive oil has solidified. If it has, allow the dressing to come to room temperature for 20 minutes and whisk again before serving.

Spicy Citrus
SALAD DRESSING

Yield: About ½ cup   *Prep time:* 5 minutes

When I lived in Toronto, I was obsessed with a local restaurant's Asian-inspired salad that came with a spicy orange salad dressing. I would order it at least once a week. The flavor of the dressing was so bright and bold. Here's my version.

⅓ cup extra-light olive oil
2 tablespoons fresh lemon juice
2 tablespoons fresh orange juice
½ teaspoon red pepper flakes
½ teaspoon fine sea salt

1. Place all the ingredients in a bowl and whisk together until combined.

2. Store the dressing in the fridge for up to 2 weeks.

3. On the day you plan on using the dressing, check to see if the olive oil has solidified. If it has, allow the dressing to come to room temperature for 20 minutes and whisk again before serving.

Homemade
AIOLI

Yield: 1 cup   *Prep time:* 15 minutes

Why aioli instead of mayo? Personally, I love aioli with all its garlicky goodness! Basic aioli is made with egg yolks, olive oil, and garlic, whereas mayo is made with egg yolks, oil, an acid like vinegar, and salt. The presence of garlic and absence of an acid are the main things that separate aioli from mayo.

1 large egg yolk

1 tablespoon Dijon mustard

1 cup extra-light olive oil

1 clove garlic, minced

Fine sea salt

1. Place the egg yolk and mustard in the bowl of a stand mixer fitted with the whisk attachment.

2. Turn the mixer to the highest speed and slowly drizzle in the olive oil, one drop at a time. Allow the olive oil to be fully mixed into the egg yolk mixture before adding more. Continue slowly adding all the olive oil until it is emulsified.

3. Add the garlic, season with salt, and stir.

4. Store the aioli in the fridge for up to 1 week.

Note: If the aioli begins to separate, spoon the mixture into a separate bowl. Start with a new egg yolk in your mixer and slowly drizzle in the old mixture until it is emulsified.

I prefer to use extra-light olive oil, sometimes called extra-light virgin olive oil, when making salad dressings and condiments like aioli because regular olive oil has a very strong taste that can be overpowering.

Smoky
CHIPOTLE AIOLI

Yield: About 1 cup   *Prep time:* 5 minutes

1 recipe Homemade Aioli (page 64)	**1.** Place all the ingredients in a small bowl and mix together.
2 teaspoons fresh lime juice	**2.** Store the aioli in the fridge for up to 1 week.
1 teaspoon ground dried chipotle pepper	
1 teaspoon smoked paprika	
8 drops of natural liquid smoke	

Extra-Garlicky
SRIRACHA AIOLI

Yield: About 1 cup   *Prep time:* 5 minutes

This sauce is made for dipping! It's spicy, creamy, and free of dairy, which makes it awesome in my view. Don't get me wrong, I love cheese, but any form of dairy besides butter really doesn't agree with me. Food should make you feel great, not icky. I use this dip for Chicken Fingers (page 232), Spicy Fish Cakes (page 212), and sometimes even Pizza (page 256).

1 recipe Homemade Aioli (page 64)	**1.** Place all the ingredients in a bowl and whisk together until combined.
2 teaspoons fresh lemon juice	**2.** Store the aioli in the fridge for up to 1 week.
2 teaspoons Sriracha sauce, homemade (page 96) or store-bought	
1 clove garlic, minced	

BASICS

SALSA

Yield: 2 cups   *Prep time:* 15 minutes   *Cook time:* 2 minutes

Here's a fresh and spicy salsa for all your Mexican-inspired meals! Don't be intimidated to make salsa from scratch. It's easy-peasy: you just pick your favorite ingredients (mine are listed below), pulse them in a food processor, and voilà, you have something to share with your loved ones.

3 large overripe tomatoes

1 jalapeño pepper, seeded and chopped

½ cup fresh cilantro leaves

¼ cup chopped red onions

4 cloves garlic, chopped

Juice of ½ lime

1 teaspoon fine sea salt

¼ teaspoon ground cumin

⅛ teaspoon ground black pepper

1. Place all the ingredients in an 8-cup food processor and pulse to the desired texture.

2. Pour into a container and serve immediately, or store in the refrigerator for up to 1 week.

Apple BUTTER

Yield: 2 cups   *Prep time:* 10 minutes   *Cook time:* 1 hour 15 minutes

Apple butter is a gift from the gods. I could eat it all day. You can also use this recipe to make applesauce: simply remove the pot from the heat when the batch starts to have the consistency of applesauce—or continue cooking to turn it into apple butter!

---

2 pounds McIntosh apples (about 6 large or 8 medium apples), peeled and chopped

3 cups water

1 cup cane sugar

1 tablespoon ground cinnamon

1 tablespoon fresh lemon juice

1 teaspoon ginger powder

½ teaspoon ground nutmeg

½ teaspoon fine sea salt

1. Place all the ingredients in a 3-quart pot and bring to a boil. Reduce the heat to medium and simmer uncovered, stirring occasionally, for 45 minutes.

2. Use a potato masher to mash the mixture until it resembles applesauce. Continue cooking until the mixture is a thick paste, about 20 minutes, stirring frequently to avoid scorching.

3. Leave the apple butter slightly chunky or use a hand blender or food processor to make it smooth.

4. Allow the apple butter to cool, then place it in a glass jar and store in the refrigerator for up to 3 months.

Apple Butter
BBQ SAUCE

Yield: About 1 cup   *Prep time:* 5 minutes   *Cook time:* 15 minutes

It's so easy to make your own barbecue sauce without questionable ingredients. There are two star ingredients in this barbecue sauce: apple butter (of course) and liquid smoke. The liquid smoke adds a depth of flavor that you can't replicate without it. Just a few drops go a long way. When I want to try new barbecue sauce flavors, I often use this recipe as a starting point but replace the apple butter with the same quantity of another ingredient, such as pureed peaches.

1 cup water

¼ cup Apple Butter (page 70)

1 tablespoon molasses

½ (6-ounce) can tomato paste (¼ cup plus 1 tablespoon)

2 tablespoons dry mustard

1 tablespoon raw apple cider vinegar

½ teaspoon onion powder

½ teaspoon garlic powder

½ teaspoon fine sea salt

¼ teaspoon natural liquid smoke, hickory flavor

1. Place all the ingredients in a mixing bowl and stir to combine. Transfer to a 1½-quart saucepan.

2. Turn the heat to high and bring to a boil. Reduce the heat to medium-low and simmer for 10 minutes, or until the sauce has thickened, stirring occasionally.

3. Store the sauce in a glass container in the refrigerator for up to 3 months.

Smoky Pineapple
BBQ SAUCE

Yield: About 2 cups   *Prep time:* 10 minutes   *Cook time:* 15 minutes

I love the sweetness the pineapple adds to this barbecue sauce. When you make your own barbecue sauce, you can avoid the high-fructose corn syrup that is so common in store-bought versions and instead use fruit and some Paleo-approved sweeteners to add sweetness to your sauce. Pureeing the pineapple also thickens the sauce.

1 cup canned pineapple chunks, drained

1 cup water

½ (6-ounce) can tomato paste (¼ cup plus 1 tablespoon)

¼ cup coconut palm sugar

¼ cup molasses

1 tablespoon raw apple cider vinegar

1½ teaspoons dry mustard

½ teaspoon ginger powder

½ teaspoon onion powder

½ teaspoon fine sea salt

¼ teaspoon natural liquid smoke, hickory flavor

1. Place all the ingredients in a 3-quart pot. Turn the heat to high and bring to a boil. Reduce the heat to medium-low and simmer for 10 minutes, or until the sauce has thickened, stirring occasionally.

2. Puree with a hand blender, or transfer the ingredients to a food processor and pulse until smooth. The sauce should be thick; if it's not as thick as you like, continue cooking until it reaches the desired consistency.

3. Store the sauce in a glass container in the refrigerator for up to 3 months.

Bone Broth

I've been making bone broth for years now, and I truly love the results. I feel that some health food trends are overhyped, but bone broth isn't one of them. When I drink bone broth on a regular basis, I see less puffiness and acne in my face and I sleep better; those are just a couple of the differences I can see and feel.

The first time I made beef bone broth, I put the marrow bones in a giant soup pot with water, veggies, and seasoning and boiled it all day. I drank the broth, but it had not gelled at all. I made it again and cooked it longer, and once again it didn't gel. It wasn't until I got some advice from a friend that I finally got my beef bone broth to gel. It was simple: use more bones, add in animal parts that contain lots of cartilage, like oxtail and feet, and then cook it in a slow cooker.

BEEF BONE BROTH

Yield: 4 quarts *Prep time:* 10 minutes *Cook time:* 48 hours

Beef bones may not be available at your local grocery store, but you can find them easily by asking your local butcher. Grass-fed beef bones are preferred, so seek out a farmer or butcher who specializes in quality meats.

2 pounds beef marrow bones and oxtails

Fine sea salt and ground black pepper

1 stalk celery, chopped

1 clove garlic, chopped

1 large onion, chopped

1 large carrot, peeled and chopped

1 tablespoon raw apple cider vinegar

Chopped fresh herbs of choice (optional)

1. Preheat the oven to 400°F. Line a rimmed baking sheet with parchment paper. Place the marrow bones and oxtails on the sheet and season with salt and pepper. Roast for 30 minutes.

2. Place the roasted bones in an 8-quart slow cooker and add the celery, garlic, onion, carrot, and vinegar. Fill with water.

3. Turn the slow cooker to low and cook for at least 48 hours.

4. Pour the broth through a strainer into a large bowl and discard the bones and vegetables.

5. Place the bowl in the refrigerator. As the broth cools, a layer of fat will form at the top, and the broth should develop the consistency of Jell-O. Use a spoon to scoop up the fat and discard it.

6. To consume the broth, reheat it over low heat until it is heated through. Add any additional flavorings at this time, such as chopped fresh parsley and salt and pepper.

7. Store leftover broth in the refrigerator for up to a week, or freeze for up to 6 months.

CHICKEN BONE BROTH

Yield: 4 quarts *Prep time:* 10 minutes *Cook time:* 24 hours

Like beef bones, chicken bones, necks, and feet may not be available at grocery stores, but they usually can be found at your local butcher. Pastured chicken bones and feet are best, so seek out a farmer or butcher who specializes in quality meats.

2 pounds chicken necks, feet, and carcasses

1 stalk celery, chopped

1 clove garlic, chopped

1 large onion, chopped

1 large carrot, chopped

1 tablespoon raw apple cider vinegar

Chopped fresh herbs of choice (optional)

Fine sea salt and ground black pepper

1. Place the bones in an 8-quart slow cooker and add the celery, garlic, onion, carrot, and vinegar. Fill with water.

2. Turn the slow cooker to low and cook for at least 24 hours.

3. Pour the broth through a strainer into a large bowl and discard the bones and vegetables.

4. Place the bowl in the refrigerator. As the broth cools, a layer of fat will form at the top, and the broth should develop the consistency of Jell-O. Use a spoon to scoop up the fat and discard it.

5. To consume the broth, reheat it over low heat until it is heated through. Add any additional flavorings at this time, such as chopped fresh parsley and salt and pepper.

Basic
CUPCAKE ICING

Yield: 1¾ cups *Prep time:* 5 minutes

This all-purpose icing recipe can be used for cupcakes and cakes. You can switch it up and make a light chocolate icing by adding 2 tablespoons of unsweetened raw cacao powder. When sourcing palm shortening, remember to purchase white shortening, not red palm oil.

1 cup palm shortening

½ cup maple syrup

¼ cup coconut cream (see page 33)

1 teaspoon vanilla extract

1. Place all the ingredients in the bowl of a stand mixer fitted with the whisk attachment. On medium speed, mix the ingredients together until combined.

2. Use immediately or store in the fridge for up to 3 weeks. When using the icing after it has been stored in the fridge, allow it to come to room temperature, then scoop the desired amount into the bowl of a stand mixer and mix on medium speed until the icing is light and fluffy again.

Chocolate
SAUCE

Yield: 2½ cups   *Prep time:* 1 minute   *Cook time:* 10 minutes

I take chocolate to the next level by adding almond butter (also known as Paleo-approved peanut butter or Paleo crack). You get a creamy chocolate sauce with a depth of flavor, and it remains soft when cool. I'm little addicted to this stuff. I smother home-made ice cream in it all summer long and use it as a chocolate topping for my Caramel Chocolate Nut Bars (page 294).

2 cups semi-sweet chocolate chips

½ cup unsweetened almond butter

1. Place the chocolate chips in the top of a double boiler over 1 inch of water. If you don't have a double boiler, you can place a heatproof glass or metal bowl over a pot filled with 1 inch of water.

2. Stir constantly over low heat until the chocolate has fully melted. Add the almond butter to the melted chocolate and mix until combined.

3. Use immediately or, once cool, store in the fridge for up to 2 weeks. Reheat on the stovetop in a pot over low heat or in the microwave in 15-second intervals.

Caramel SAUCE

Yield: 1 cup *Prep time:* 5 minutes *Cook time:* 20 minutes

I thought that a dairy-free caramel sauce was impossible, like a pot of gold at the end of a rainbow—you want to believe that it exists, but it feels like a fairy tale. Then I had a breakthrough. When I made the first version of this sauce for my dessert cookbook, *Indulge*, it occurred to me that if I replaced heavy cream with coconut cream, I'd have a dairy-free caramel sauce. The result was not only made with real ingredients but also effortless to make. This recipe results in a thick caramel sauce that remains soft when cool.

1 cup coconut palm sugar

½ cup coconut cream (see page 33)

¼ teaspoon fine sea salt

1. Mix all the ingredients together in a 1½-quart saucepan. Turn the heat to high, whisking constantly. Once the sauce comes to a boil, lower the heat to medium and continue whisking constantly. The sauce is done when it is thick and light brown in color.

2. Take the pan off the heat and pour the mixture into a heatproof glass container, like a mason jar. Use immediately or let cool and store in the refrigerator for up to 2 weeks.

3. Reheat on the stovetop in a pot over low heat or in the microwave in 15-second intervals. The oil may separate when the sauce is reheated. If that happens, use a whisk to mix it together again.

Coconut Flour
BAR BASE

Yield: One 8-inch square bar crust or one 9-inch round pie or tart crust

Prep time: 10 minutes *Cook time:* 15 minutes

This nut-free dough can be used in place of nut flour–based crusts for bars, pies, and tarts.

¼ cup coconut oil

2 tablespoons raw honey

4 large eggs

½ cup full-fat coconut milk

1¼ cups sifted coconut flour

½ cup arrowroot starch

¼ teaspoon fine sea salt

1. Preheat the oven to 350°F. Grease a 9-inch pie or tart pan or line an 8-inch square baking pan with parchment paper.

2. In a medium-sized bowl, cream the coconut oil and honey until smooth and well mixed.

3. Add the eggs and mix until smooth. Then add the coconut milk and mix until smooth. Add the coconut flour, arrowroot starch, and salt and mix until well incorporated.

4. Press the dough into the prepared pan. Poke the bottom of the dough with a fork to allow steam to escape and keep the crust flat.

5. Bake for 15 minutes, or until the crust is slightly golden and feels firm to the touch.

Fermented FOODS & DRINKS

Fermentation 101

I love fermenting foods and beverages. I firmly believe that fermented foods are fundamental for a healthy lifestyle. They support beneficial bacteria in the gut, and that leads to improved digestion and better absorption of nutrients. There's also some evidence that a better balance of bacteria in the gut can help with autoimmune disorders and allergies, improve mood, and assist with weight loss. The recipes in this chapter are simple and will help to get you started with fermented foods and drinks.

Fermentation **IS RIGHT UP THERE** WITH **COOKING** **AS ONE OF THE MOST POWERFUL METHODS** TO **TRANSFORM** *food.*

—JOHN DURANT,
The Paleo Manifesto: Ancient Wisdom for Lifelong Health

WHAT IS FERMENTATION?

Fermentation is the process of using bacteria to convert sugar or starch into an acid or alcohol. That's why fermented drinks like kombucha start off with high amounts of sugar but have significantly less by the time they are done fermenting. The process of fermentation makes the food or drink easier to digest and increases its shelf life. Wine, yogurt, brie cheese, and beer are all examples of fermented beverages and foods.

There are three types of fermentation:

- *Lactic acid fermentation, also known as lacto-fermentation:* Despite the name, lacto-fermented recipes do not need dairy to ferment. *Lacto* here refers to a specific kind of beneficial bacteria called *lactobacillus*. Cabbage is naturally covered in lactobacillus, and when you add salt, you create an environment that allows lactobacillus to flourish and kills bad bacteria. The sauerkraut and yogurt recipes in this book also use lacto-fermentation.

- *Ethyl alcohol fermentation:* Think of this as yeast fermentation. Yeast consumes the sugar in the drink and turns it into alcohol—beer and wine both use this kind of fermentation. Kombucha and ginger bug (the base for many traditional sodas) are examples of ethyl alcohol fermentation and acetic fermentation (see below) working together.

- *Acetic fermentation:* This type of fermentation uses the airborne bacteria acetobacter to convert alcohol into acetic acid and is often used to make vinegars. During fermentation, kombucha and ginger bug are covered with cloth instead of a lid to allow acetobacter bacteria into the drink.

THE BENEFITS OF FERMENTATION

- *It increases levels of minerals and vitamins:* For example, fermenting cabbage increases its levels of vitamin C dramatically. In fact, sauerkraut helped prevent scurvy in sailors on long voyages.

- *It aids in digestion:* During the fermentation process, bacteria feed on the sugar or starch in the food or drink. This both decreases the sugar in the fermented food and provides you with enzymes that help you digest your food better.

- *It provides us with probiotics:* The fermentation process adds probiotics to foods, and these can replace expensive store-bought probiotics. Different fermented foods are known for having different probiotic strains.

- *It increases shelf life:* Homemade sauerkraut (pages 90 and 92) can last for at least six months. Condiments like homemade mayo and salsa that have been fermented last weeks longer than their homemade unfermented versions.

HOW TO FERMENT

Each fermented food is made slightly differently (see the recipes in this chapter for instructions), but there are some common elements needed for all fermented foods and drinks.

Culture: Some foods, like sauerkraut (pages 90 and 92), can be fermented with just water and salt, whereas yogurt (page 112) and kombucha (page 100) rely on a starter culture.

Temperature: 65°F to 75°F works great for most types of fermenting. If it's winter and it's cold in your home, fermentation is usually slower; as a result, you will need to increase the fermentation time. During the warmer months of summer, items typically ferment more quickly. Refrigerating fermented foods will halt the fermentation process. Kombucha ferments at a higher temperature.

Filtered water: Fermentation recipes use filtered water rather than tap water because the chlorine in tap water can kill the good bacteria you are trying to grow.

EQUIPMENT FOR FERMENTING

Glass jars: I save glass jars and lids of all different sizes and use them for various fermented foods. If you get into fermenting, you can purchase glass jars made specifically for fermenting. Never use plastic jars: the plastic can leach into what you are fermenting.

Glass fermentation weights: These are used to keep the food submerged below the liquid in the jar. Glass fermentation weights can be purchased on Amazon. I often use a small ceramic condiment bowl instead of weights. It works just as well.

Bottles: Swing-top bottles are best for any fermented drink. You can purchase them anywhere, including Amazon. You can also use wine bottles and corks to bottle kombucha, but you will need a wine corker to properly insert the cork.

STERILIZING YOUR EQUIPMENT

Some fermentation books insist you sterilize all the equipment that will be used in the fermentation process, including any spoons, knives, jars, and lids that will come into contact with the product you will be fermenting. This controls what bacteria will flourish when you ferment. I prefer to just wash all my equipment in the dishwasher, which sanitizes to my satisfaction. But if you want to sterilize your equipment by hand, bring water to a boil (212°F) in a pot that is large enough to hold your largest bottle or jar. Place your equipment in the pot and boil for at least 20 minutes, making sure that it remains submerged.

Raw SAUERKRAUT

Yield: 1 quart   *Prep time:* 25 minutes, not including fermentation time

I learned how to make fermented foods after reading *Real Food Fermentation* by Alex Lewin. His book opened my eyes to the idea of preserving foods with beneficial bacteria. Fermenting foods is not complicated, and of all the foods, sauerkraut is the easiest to make.

2 pounds cabbage (about ½ head), core removed

1 tablespoon plus 1 teaspoon fine sea salt

Filtered water

1. Remove the outer cabbage leaves that are old and damaged.

2. Use a knife, food processor, or mandoline to cut the cabbage into very thin slices.

3. Place the sliced cabbage in a very large bowl and sprinkle with the salt. Massage the cabbage with your hands to soften it. Keep massaging until you can take a handful of cabbage and squeeze water out of it, about 15 minutes.

4. Start packing the cabbage into a 1-quart (1-liter) wide-mouth canning jar. Pack it a quarter of the way and then use a utensil to compress it, then add more cabbage and repeat until all the cabbage is in the jar. Pour the water left in the bowl into the jar. If the cabbage is not covered with cabbage water, add enough filtered water to completely cover the cabbage. Make sure that there is about 1 inch of space between the top of the cabbage and the mouth of the jar, because the cabbage will expand as it ferments.

5. Ferment the sauerkraut for at least 7 days. Place the jar in a dark space with a tray under it to catch any liquid that flows out. The room in which you ferment the sauerkraut needs to be warm, ideally 65°F to 75°F. Do not ferment the sauerkraut in your basement or root cellar. Each day, unscrew the lid, push the cabbage back under the liquid, and check for mold. If you see mold, discard the moldy area. You can tell that the sauerkraut is fermenting when there are bubbles at the top of the jar.

6. The sauerkraut is done when you like the flavor. Taste after 7 days; if you want it to have a more sour taste, ferment it longer.

7. Store the sauerkraut in your fridge. It will last for at least 6 months.

Rainbow
SAUERKRAUT

Yield: 1 quart   *Prep time:* 25 minutes, not including fermentation time

With its beautiful orange and purple colors and rich beet taste, this is sauerkraut taken to the next level.

---

1 pound cabbage (about ¼ head), core removed

1 large carrot, peeled and shredded

1 red beet, peeled and shredded

1 tablespoon plus 1 teaspoon fine sea salt

Filtered water

1. Remove the outer cabbage leaves that are old and damaged.

2. Use a knife, food processor, or mandoline to cut the cabbage into very thin slices.

3. Place the sliced cabbage, carrot, and beet in a very large bowl and sprinkle with the salt. Massage the mixture with your hands to soften it. Keep massaging until you can take a handful and squeeze water out of it, about 15 minutes.

4. Start packing the cabbage mixture into a 1-quart (1-liter) wide-mouth canning jar. Pack it a quarter of the way and then use a utensil to compress it, then add more cabbage mixture and repeat until all the mixture is in the jar. Pour the water left in the bowl into the jar. If the cabbage mixture is not covered by the cabbage water, add enough filtered water to completely cover the cabbage. Make sure that there is about 1 inch of space between the top of the cabbage mixture and the mouth of the jar, because the cabbage mixture will expand as it ferments. Seal with a lid.

5. Ferment the sauerkraut for at least 7 days. Place the jar in a dark space with a tray under it to catch any liquid that flows out. The room in which you ferment the sauerkraut needs to be warm, ideally 65°F to 75°F. Do not ferment the sauerkraut in your basement or root cellar. Each day, unscrew the lid, push the cabbage mixture back under the liquid, and check for mold. If you see any mold, discard the moldy area. You can tell that the sauerkraut is fermenting when there are bubbles at the top of the jar.

6. The sauerkraut is done when you like the flavor. Taste after 7 days; if you want it to have a more sour taste, ferment it longer.

7. Store the sauerkraut in your fridge. It will last for at least 6 months.

Fermented
JALAPEÑO PEPPERS

Yield: 1 cup *Prep time:* 10 minutes, not including fermentation time

This is an easy way to store an abundance of jalapeño peppers for later use. Plus, by fermenting them, you are adding healthy probiotics. The probiotics are only beneficial when the peppers are consumed cold—for example, as a topping on a taco. If they're heated, the probiotics will be killed.

6 jalapeño peppers, stems removed, cut crosswise into ¼-inch slices

1 teaspoon fine sea salt

Filtered water

1. Place all the ingredients in an 8-ounce jar and fill with filtered water.

2. Insert a fermentation weight or small glass or ceramic bowl to weigh down the peppers. Seal tightly with a lid.

3. Store the jar in a dark area at room temperature, ideally 65°F to 75°F. Do not ferment the peppers in your basement or root cellar.

4. Check the peppers daily. The liquid will start to bubble, and the jalapeños will soften. They will be done fermenting in 4 to 7 days. (Note: The photo shows the peppers after 1 day of fermentation.)

5. Store the peppers in the fridge. They will last for at least 6 months.

Fermented
SRIRACHA SAUCE

Yield: 2½ cups   *Prep time:* 10 minutes, not including fermentation time   *Cook time:* 25 minutes

Traditional Sriracha sauces are made from red serrano chiles, but these peppers are available for only a short time during the year. My version uses a combination of easy-to-find peppers to create a similar-tasting sauce.

10 Scotch bonnet chiles, chopped (remove seeds if you want a milder sauce)

6 habanero chiles, chopped (remove seeds if you want a milder sauce)

1 red bell pepper, chopped

1 cup coconut palm sugar

1 cup filtered water

½ cup tomato paste

4 cloves garlic, chopped

1 tablespoon plus 1 teaspoon fine sea salt

½ cup raw apple cider vinegar

1. Place all the ingredients except the vinegar in a food processor and puree until smooth.

2. Pour the mixture into a 1½-quart pot and bring to a boil. Reduce the heat to medium and cook for 20 minutes to help develop the flavors.

3. Allow the mixture to cool to room temperature, then add the vinegar and stir to combine.

4. Pour the sauce into a 3-cup or larger jar. Place a cloth over the top and secure with elastic.

5. Leave the sauce out on the counter to ferment for 4 to 7 days. You may see bubbles form at the top of the jar; this is part of the fermentation process. The longer you let it ferment, the stronger the flavor will be.

6. Once the sauce is fermented to your liking, pour into a condiment bottle and store in the refrigerator for up to 6 months.

Garlic Dill PICKLES

Yield: 1 quart *Prep time:* 10 minutes, not including fermentation time

My first job when I was in college studying marketing was at the local pickle factory. I started on the production line. My job was to push the pickles into the glass jars as they went down the line. My thumbs were so sore after an eight-hour day. Since summer is the main growing season for cucumbers, we worked six or seven days a week for the whole summer. When I came back the following summer, I was immediately promoted to working in the lab, testing batches of pickles, sauerkraut, and eggs (pickled eggs are the most foul-smelling things!). I didn't know it then, but I've since learned from the holistic community that fermenting and pickling cucumbers at the same time can create a probiotic-rich food in a few days.

8 to 10 pickling cucumbers

6 sprigs fresh dill, enough to cover bottom of jar

6 cloves garlic, peeled

2 tablespoons fine sea salt

Filtered water

1. Wash the cucumbers. Cut the blossom end off of each cucumber (not the end that was attached to the stem).

2. Place the dill in a 1-quart (1-liter) glass jar, then add the garlic.

3. Neatly place the whole cucumbers in the jar. (Note: Keep the cucumbers whole. If you cut them into spears, they will become mushy during fermentation.) Sprinkle the salt over the cucumbers. Fill the jar with filtered water until the cucumbers are covered.

4. Screw the lid on tightly and place the jar in a dark area away from direct sunlight. Place the jar on a tray to catch any juices that overflow from the bottle during the fermentation process. Make sure to put the jar in a room that is warm, ideally 65°F to 75°F. Do not ferment the pickles in your basement or root cellar. The warmth of the room will affect how fast the pickles ferment.

5. Each day, unscrew the lid and push down any pickles that have popped up, or use a glass fermentation weight or small ceramic or glass bowl to keep the pickles down. It is important that the pickles stay under the brine so they don't grow mold. You can tell that your pickles are fermenting when you see bubbles on the surface of the brine.

6. Taste the pickles after 3 days. When they have reached your desired crunchiness and flavor, place the jar in the fridge. The pickles will last for 2 weeks.

KOMBUCHA

Yield: 1¼ gallons *Prep time:* 2 hours, not including fermentation time

Kombucha is my favorite fermented drink. I practically live on this stuff and go through withdrawal if I'm on vacation and can't get a hold of it. Kombucha is full of healthy bacteria and yeast, as well as healthy acids that support liver function to help remove toxins from the body. This tutorial on how to make kombucha produces more than a gallon. See my notes at the end of the recipe to learn how to adjust the recipe for a smaller batch, as well as how to build up the starter tea.

1 gallon filtered water

4 bags green tea

1 cup cane sugar

4 cups starter tea (see Note)

1 large SCOBY (4 to 6 inches in diameter and ¼ to ½ inch thick; see Note)

Special equipment:

2-gallon glass water jug with spigot

4 (1-quart) swing-top bottles

1. Place the water in a large pot and bring to a boil.

2. Add the tea bags to the boiling water. Turn off the heat and steep for about 20 minutes. Remove the tea bags.

3. Add the sugar to the tea and stir to dissolve.

4. Cool the brew to room temperature. This step is imperative: adding a hot liquid to the starter tea and SCOBY will kill the probiotics and the SCOBY.

5. Pour the cooled sweetened green tea into a 2-gallon glass water jug with a spigot. Add the starter tea to the jug. Cover the jug with a clean, tightly woven cloth and hold it tightly in place with an elastic. Never leave the jar uncovered or even loosely covered because fruit flies will get into your batch. If you ever find fruit flies in your batch, discard it.

6. Place the jug in a warm, darkened or sunlit room, ideally between 75°F and 85°F; 78°F to 80°F is the sweet spot. Do not ferment kombucha in your basement or root cellar. If the environment is too cold, it can cause mold to grow.

7. During the warmer months or in temperate climates, it typically takes 7 to 10 days for a batch to be ready; in the winter, the fermentation time increases to 14 to 21 days. Start tasting your batch after 3 days. When it is ready, the liquid will fizz as you pour it into a glass. The taste will change from sweet tea to tart overnight. If you don't know what plain kombucha tastes like, I recommend that you purchase a few bottles at your local store so you have a reference point.

8. To bottle your kombucha, pour it into four 1-quart swing-top bottles and cap the bottles. Save 4 cups for your next batch. Store the kombucha in your fridge or root cellar. Kombucha lasts forever; however, the taste will change and the kombucha may turn into kombucha vinegar if left too long.

9. You can increase the carbonation in your capped bottles of kombucha by fermenting them for 3 more days at room temperature.

Note: *If you are just starting out and do not have a large SCOBY or enough starter tea to make the recipe, you will need to build up the size of your SCOBY and your amount of starter tea. To build up from 1 cup of starter tea, start by brewing 1 quart of sweetened green tea (use 2 to 4 bags and ¼ cup of sugar per 1 quart of water), then once it's cool, add the starter tea and SCOBY and ferment according to the recipe. Reserve 2 cups of the finished kombucha as starter tea, and for the next batch, make ½ gallon (8 cups) of brewed green tea and add the 2 cups of starter tea. From that batch of finished kombucha, reserve 4 cups as starter tea—you can use this to make the recipe.*

Just remember that when you're making kombucha, the ratio is always one part starter tea (and SCOBY) to four parts freshly made sweetened green tea.

Terminology & Tips:

SCOBY: *An acronym coined by Len Porzio, SCOBY stands for Symbiotic Culture of Bacteria and Yeast. The SCOBY is the white, alien-looking thing floating at the top of the jar. This yeast ferments the sugar by breaking it down from a disaccharide to monosaccharides. The by-products of this process fuel the bacteria to create healthy acids. The bacteria increase the benefit of the tea by making its elements more bioavailable and increasing the amount of antioxidants naturally present in the tea.*

Starter tea: *If you buy a SCOBY or receive one from a friend, you will get at least 1 cup of tea. This tea is considered your starter tea. The tea came from the same batch as the SCOBY and contains the beneficial bacteria to aid in the fermentation. It is important to add the starter tea as the last ingredient in your kombucha because its low pH serves as a protective barrier, preventing other microorganisms from colonizing the brew.*

Each batch of kombucha creates a new baby SCOBY. You can leave the SCOBY attached to the original SCOBY (referred to as "the mother"), discard the new SCOBY, give it to a friend, or keep it as a backup by placing it in a jar with enough kombucha to start a new batch and storing it at room temperature.

Sugar: *Don't use artificial sugar or raw honey. You must use real cane sugar. The antibacterial properties of raw honey will not work with kombucha's fermentation process. Real sugar feeds the yeast, and by the time the kombucha has fermented, most of the sugar will have been consumed by the yeast.*

Watermelon Kiwi
KOMBUCHA

Yield: 1 quart   *Prep time:* 5 minutes, not including fermentation time

Kiwi has a unique sour flavor that I love when combined with the light, refreshing taste of watermelon. This drink is perfect for a hot summer day. For a fancy presentation, garnish glasses of this kombucha with cubed watermelon and sliced kiwi, as shown in the photo.

¼ cup seeded and finely chopped watermelon

¼ cup peeled and finely chopped kiwi

3 cups Kombucha (page 100)

Special equipment:

1 (1-quart) swing-top bottle

1. Use a funnel to push the watermelon and kiwi into a 1-quart (1-liter) swing-top bottle. Add the kombucha and cap the bottle.

2. Ferment at room temperature for 3 days. Be careful when opening the bottle, as it will have built up carbon dioxide.

3. After fermenting, store the kombucha in the fridge indefinitely.

Strawberry Basil
KOMBUCHA

Yield: 1 quart   *Prep time:* 5 minutes, not including fermentation time

This has become my favorite flavored kombucha. The strawberry flavor is refreshing and light, and then you get an amazing hit of pungent sweet basil! I love how just two ingredients can have such an impact on taste.

3 strawberries, stems removed, finely chopped

3 fresh basil leaves, chopped

2 tablespoons fresh lemon juice

3 cups Kombucha (page 100)

Special equipment:

1 (1-quart) swing-top bottle

1. Use a funnel to push the strawberries and basil into a 1-quart (1-liter) swing-top bottle. Add the lemon juice and kombucha and cap the bottle.

2. Ferment at room temperature for 3 days. Be careful when opening the bottle, as it will have built up carbon dioxide.

3. After fermenting, store the kombucha in the fridge indefinitely.

Berry Ginger
KOMBUCHA

Yield: 1 quart   *Prep time:* 5 minutes, not including fermentation time

This is a fun berry-flavored kombucha drink with a hint of ginger. I prefer to use whole fruit rather than fruit juice to flavor my kombucha.

¼ cup blackberries, chopped

¼ cup blueberries, chopped

2 tablespoons peeled and finely chopped fresh ginger

3 cups Kombucha (page 100)

Mixed berries, for garnish (optional)

Special equipment:

1 (1-quart) swing-top bottle

1. Use a funnel to push the berries and ginger into a 1-quart (1-liter) swing-top bottle. Add the kombucha and cap the bottle.

2. Ferment at room temperature for 3 days. Be careful when opening the bottle, as it will have built up carbon dioxide. When serving, you can strain out the fruit or leave it in.

3. After fermenting, garnish with mixed berries, if desired, and serve. Store the kombucha in the fridge indefinitely.

Ginger BUG

Yield: 1 cup *Prep time:* 5 minutes, not including fermentation time

Ginger bugs are the bases for fermented root beers, fruit-based sodas, and ginger ale. The fermented mixture of sugar and ginger is referred to as a "bug." The bug relies on wild yeast and bacteria to form, and the yeast and bacteria feed on the sugar. Using organic ginger is extremely important in this recipe. I have heard of many people's ginger bug not working because they didn't use organic ginger.

2 tablespoons plus at least 7 tablespoons peeled and finely chopped organic fresh ginger, divided

2 tablespoons plus at least 7 tablespoons cane sugar, divided

1 cup plus at least 7 tablespoons filtered water, divided

1. Place 2 tablespoons of the ginger, 2 tablespoons of the cane sugar, and 1 cup of the water in a 2-cup (500 ml) mason jar.

2. Use a paper towel or clean cloth to cover the opening of the jar and secure with an elastic. Store the jar in a dark place.

3. Every day, add 1 tablespoon of ginger, 1 tablespoon of sugar, and 1 tablespoon of filtered water and stir. After 7 days, your bug should be ready to use to make soda (see page 110 for a recipe). The bug will smell yeasty, be cloudy and bubbling, and have the consistency of a thick syrup.

4. You can continue to feed the bug by repeating Step 3, or place the bug in the fridge and feed it once a week for maintenance. To use the bug after refrigerating, start feeding it daily and store it in a dark place at room temperature. In about a week, the top should get bubbly again. If not, keep feeding it daily. The bug is ready to use when you see bubbles on the top.

5. If you see mold on your bug, remove the mold. If the mold returns, discard the bug.

6. To use the ginger bug, strain off ¼ cup of the liquid per 1 quart of liquid specified in the recipe.

7. Replace any ginger bug liquid that has been used with ¼ cup filtered water and 2 tablespoons sugar.

Cherry Ginger SODA

Yield: 3¼ cups *Prep time:* 5 minutes, not including fermentation time

This is a healthier way to drink soda that provides your body with beneficial bacteria. The microorganisms consume the sugar in the cherry juice and create carbon dioxide. Since the swing-top bottle is sealed for three days, carbon dioxide builds up and creates a fizzy drink. You can use any juice you like in this recipe, but always use ¼ cup of strained Ginger Bug liquid for every 3 cups of juice.

3 cups tart cherry juice
¼ cup strained Ginger Bug liquid (page 108)

Special equipment:
1 (1-quart) swing-top bottle

1. In a large bowl, whisk together the ingredients. Pour into a 1-quart (1-liter) swing-top bottle and allow to ferment at room temperature for 3 days.

2. After fermenting, store the soda in the fridge indefinitely. Be careful when opening the bottle, as it will have built up carbon dioxide.

Coconut Milk
YOGURT

Yield: 1 quart *Prep time:* 45 minutes *Cook time:* 8 to 24 hours

Coconut milk makes a great dairy-free yogurt, but to have successful results, you need to add a little sugar for the bacteria to feed on during fermentation, and you need to use a thickener like gelatin. I assure you, the addition of gelatin does not turn it into yogurt Jell-O!

2 (13½-ounce) cans full-fat coconut milk

2 teaspoons grass-fed unflavored gelatin

1 tablespoon maple syrup

3 probiotic pills (25 billion CFU or above each) or ¼ cup coconut milk yogurt starter (from previous batch)

Special equipment:

Yogurt maker

1. In a 1-quart pot, heat the milk until it reaches 180°F. Turn off the heat and allow the milk cool to 105°F.

2. Scoop ¼ cup of the heated milk into a measuring cup and whisk in the gelatin. Return the gelatin mixture to the rest of the milk.

3. Whisk in the maple syrup. Open the probiotic pills and whisk in the powder, or whisk in the yogurt starter.

4. Pour the mixture into the jars that came with your yogurt maker. Turn on the yogurt maker and ferment for 8 to 24 hours. The longer you ferment it, the more sour it will taste.

5. The finished yogurt will have separated into a liquid and a solid. This is normal. Stir to recombine, then place in the fridge for at least 8 hours. After 8 hours, the yogurt will be thick.

6. Serve the yogurt plain or with your favorite garnishes, like raw honey, fruit, and/or cinnamon.

7. Store the yogurt in the fridge for up to 2 weeks. Remember to save ¼ cup as a starter for your next batch.

Note: If you would like to make yogurt with cow's milk, goat's milk, or sheep's milk, use organic milk from pastured animals and follow the same instructions but omit the gelatin and maple syrup, and if you use a starter, make sure it's made from the same kind of milk. You can make the yogurt lactose-free by fermenting it for 24 hours.

CHAPTER 3

Crackers, Wraps, BREADS, BAGELS & MUFFINS

Vegetable CRACKERS

Yield: 50 crackers Prep time: 10 minutes Cook time: 15 minutes

A savory blend of garlic, onions, peppers, and carrots with a flirty spiciness, these crunchy crackers are waiting to be the delivery vehicles for pâté, kielbasa, or raw grass-fed cheese.

1 cup almond flour

½ cup arrowroot starch

2½ tablespoons water

2 tablespoons extra-virgin olive oil

¼ teaspoon fine sea salt

¼ cup finely chopped red bell peppers

¼ cup finely shredded carrots

¼ cup finely chopped jalapeño peppers (remove seeds for less heat)

1 tablespoon plus 1 teaspoon dried chopped onions

2 teaspoons dried minced garlic

2 teaspoons dried parsley

FOR THE BUTTERY TOPPING:

1 tablespoon ghee (page 56), melted

½ teaspoon fine sea salt

1. Preheat the oven to 400°F.

2. In a small bowl, combine the almond flour, arrowroot starch, water, olive oil, and salt. Use either your hands or a hand mixer to mix until a dough forms.

3. Mix the red bell peppers, carrots, jalapeños, onions, garlic, and parsley into the dough.

4. Place the dough between two pieces of parchment paper. Using a rolling pin, roll the dough until it is ⅛ inch thick. Remove the top piece of parchment paper.

5. Mix together the ingredients for the topping and use a pastry brush to brush the mixture all over the top of the dough. Cut the dough into 1-by-2-inch rectangles.

6. Slide the parchment paper with the dough onto a large baking sheet.

7. Bake for 15 minutes, or until golden brown and firm to the touch. If you find that the outer crackers are becoming golden before the middle crackers are done, remove the outer crackers from the baking sheet and continue baking until the rest of the crackers are done. Allow the crackers to cool on the baking sheet.

8. Store the crackers in an airtight container at room temperature for up to 2 days.

"Whole-Grain" CRACKERS

Yield: 22 crackers   *Prep time:* 5 minutes   *Cook time:* 10 minutes

These easy-to-make crackers taste like classic salty crackers and pair well with pâté or other spreads. They get their "whole-grain" texture from a combination of sliced almonds, chia seeds, and sunflower seeds.

1 cup almond flour

½ cup arrowroot starch

2½ tablespoons water

2 tablespoons extra-virgin olive oil

½ teaspoon fine sea salt

¼ teaspoon ground black pepper

2 tablespoons sliced almonds

2 tablespoons chia seeds

2 tablespoons sunflower seeds

1. Preheat the oven to 400°F.

2. In a small bowl, combine the almond flour, arrowroot starch, water, olive oil, salt, and pepper. Use either your hands or a hand mixer to mix until a dough forms.

3. Mix the sliced almonds, chia seeds, and sunflower seeds into the dough.

4. Place the dough between two pieces of parchment paper. Using a rolling pin, roll the dough until it is ⅛ inch thick. Remove the top piece of parchment paper.

5. Cut dough into 2-inch squares.

6. Slide the parchment paper with the dough onto a baking sheet.

7. Bake for 10 minutes, or until light brown and firm to the touch. If you find that the outer crackers are becoming golden before the middle crackers are done, remove the outer crackers from the baking sheet and continue baking until the rest of the crackers are done. Allow the crackers to cool on the baking sheet.

8. Store the crackers in an airtight container at room temperature for up to 2 days.

"Everything Bagel"-Inspired
CRACKERS

Yield: 50 crackers   *Prep time:* 5 minutes   *Cook time:* 10 minutes

These crackers are reminiscent of one of my favorite bagels when I was a kid. They are crisp, light, and very yummy.

---

1 cup almond flour

½ cup arrowroot starch

2½ tablespoons water

2 tablespoons extra-virgin olive oil

2 teaspoons dried onion flakes

2 teaspoons poppy seeds

2 teaspoons white sesame seeds

1 teaspoon dried minced garlic

1 teaspoon sea salt

FOR THE BUTTERY TOPPING:

1 tablespoon ghee (page 56), melted

½ teaspoon fine sea salt

1. Preheat the oven to 400°F.

2. In a small bowl, combine all the ingredients for the crackers. Use either your hands or a hand mixer to mix until a dough forms.

3. Place the dough between two pieces of parchment paper. Using a rolling pin, roll the dough until it is ⅛ inch thick. Remove the top piece of parchment paper.

4. Mix together the ingredients for the topping and use a pastry brush to brush the topping all over the top of the dough.

5. Cut the dough into 1-by-2-inch rectangles.

6. Slide the parchment paper with the dough onto a baking sheet.

7. Bake for 10 minutes, or until light brown and firm to the touch. If you find that the outer crackers are becoming golden before the middle crackers are done, remove the outer crackers from the baking sheet and continue baking until the rest of the crackers are done. Allow the crackers to cool on the baking sheet.

8. Store the crackers in an airtight container at room temperature for up to 2 days.

Banana MUFFINS

Yield: 10 muffins   *Prep time:* 20 minutes   *Cook time:* 30 minutes

Here's a simple banana muffin recipe that you can customize by adding chocolate chips, walnuts, or raisins. The coconut flour makes these muffins nut-free and very light.

4 large eggs, separated

¼ cup maple syrup

1 teaspoon cream of tartar

1 cup mashed ripe banana

½ cup coconut oil

½ cup plus 2 tablespoons sifted coconut flour

¼ cup arrowroot starch

1½ teaspoons ground cinnamon

1 teaspoon ginger powder

½ teaspoon ground allspice

¼ teaspoon ground nutmeg

¾ teaspoon baking soda

½ teaspoon fine sea salt

1 teaspoon fresh lemon juice

1. Preheat oven to 350°F. Line a 12-well muffin pan with 10 liners.

2. In a large metal or glass bowl, use a hand mixer to whip the egg whites, maple syrup, and cream of tartar until stiff peaks form.

3. In a separate bowl, cream the egg yolks, banana, and coconut oil until evenly combined.

4. Place the coconut flour, arrowroot starch, spices, baking soda, and salt in a bowl and whisk to combine. Then add the dry ingredients and the lemon juice to the wet ingredients and mix until smooth.

5. With the mixer running, slowly add the mixture to the whipped egg whites, mixing until well combined. Spoon the batter into the lined muffin cups, filling them to the top.

6. Bake for 30 minutes, or until the tops are firm to the touch and a toothpick inserted into the middle of a muffin comes out clean.

7. Allow the muffins to cool in the pan for 5 minutes, then move them to a cooling rack to cool completely.

8. Store the muffins in an airtight container at room temperature for up to 2 days, or store in the freezer for up to 3 months.

Fruit Jam MUFFINS

Yield: 12 muffins   *Prep time:* 15 minutes   *Cook time:* 40 minutes

These muffins are inspired by what used to be my favorite muffin at Tim Hortons, the go-to place in Canada for coffee and treats like doughnuts and muffins. They sell a muffin called the Fruit Explosion that is bursting with a delicious fruit jam filling and chunks of fruit, like apples and berries. I've simplified the recipe with a mixed fruit jam that is easy to make.

FOR THE FRUIT JAM FILLING:

½ medium green apple (any variety), peeled and finely chopped
½ cup frozen mixed berries
2 tablespoons raw honey
1 tablespoon arrowroot starch
½ teaspoon fresh lemon juice

FOR THE BATTER:

8 large eggs, separated
2 teaspoons cream of tartar
½ cup coconut oil
¼ cup raw honey
1 teaspoon vanilla extract
½ cup sifted coconut flour
½ cup arrowroot starch
½ teaspoon baking soda
½ teaspoon fine sea salt
1 ripe banana, thinly sliced

1. Make the fruit jam filling first so that it can cool while you make the batter: Place all the jam ingredients in a medium-sized pot over medium-low heat. Cook, stirring constantly, for 10 minutes, then increase the heat to medium and continue to cook, stirring occasionally, until the mixture thickens, about 10 minutes more. When the consistency is similar to that of jam, take the pot off the heat.

2. Preheat the oven to 350°F. Line a 12-well muffin pan with liners.

3. Make the muffin batter: In a large glass or metal bowl, combine the egg whites and cream of tartar. Use a hand mixer to whip the egg whites until stiff peaks form.

4. In a separate bowl, cream the coconut oil and honey. Add the egg yolks and vanilla and mix well.

5. In a separate bowl, whisk together the sifted coconut flour, arrowroot starch, baking soda, and salt. Then add it to the egg yolk mixture and mix until smooth. Slowly mix the egg yolk mixture into the whipped egg whites.

6. Spoon the batter into the lined muffin cups, filling each cup halfway. Place 1 heaping teaspoon of the jam mixture in the center of each muffin. Spoon the remaining batter on top of the muffins, filling them to just below the rim. Top each muffin with 2 or 3 banana slices.

7. Bake for 15 to 20 minutes, until the tops are firm to the touch and a toothpick comes out clean. Allow the muffins to cool in the pan for 5 minutes, then move them to a cooling rack to cool completely.

8. Store the muffins at room temperature in an airtight container for up to 2 days, or store in the freezer for up to 3 months.

Morning Glory MUFFINS

Yield: 12 muffins   *Prep time:* 15 minutes   *Cook time:* 30 minutes

These muffins are like carrot muffins, but they're jam-packed with even more goodies, like seeds and dried fruit. They are light in texture and aren't overly sweet, making them great for snacking.

6 large eggs, separated

1 teaspoon cream of tartar

¼ cup coconut oil

¼ cup maple syrup

½ cup arrowroot starch

¼ cup plus 1 tablespoon sifted coconut flour

1½ teaspoons ground cinnamon

1 teaspoon ground ginger

½ teaspoon ground allspice

¼ teaspoon ground nutmeg

¾ teaspoon baking soda

½ teaspoon fine sea salt

1 teaspoon fresh lemon juice

1 cup grated carrots

½ cup peeled and grated apples (any variety)

½ cup drained crushed pineapple

½ cup unsweetened shredded coconut

½ cup raisins

½ cup unsweetened dried cranberries

½ cup sunflower seeds

1. Preheat the oven to 350°F. Line a 12-well muffin pan with liners.

2. In a large metal or glass bowl, use a hand mixer to whip the egg whites and cream of tartar until stiff peaks form.

3. In a separate bowl, cream the egg yolks, coconut oil, and maple syrup.

4. In a third bowl, whisk together the arrowroot starch, coconut flour, spices, baking soda, and salt. Add the flour mixture and lemon juice to the egg yolk mixture and mix until combined.

5. With the hand mixer on low speed, slowly add the egg yolk mixture to the whipped egg whites and mix until well combined.

6. Use paper towels to blot the carrots, apples, and pineapple until most of the moisture is removed. Stir the coconut, raisins, cranberries, sunflower seeds, carrots, apple, and pineapple into the batter.

7. Pour the batter into the muffin cups, filling them to the top.

8. Bake for 25 to 30 minutes, until the tops are firm to the touch and a toothpick inserted into the middle of a muffin comes out clean. Let cool in the pan for 5 minutes, then transfer to a wire rack to cool completely.

9. Store the muffins in an airtight container at room temperature for up to 2 days, or freeze for up to 3 months.

Paleo BREAD

Yield: One 8-by-4-inch loaf   Prep time: 5 minutes   Cook time: 50 minutes

This light and fluffy Paleo bread tastes amazing! After months of trial and error to get the ratio of starch, fat, and liquid correct, I came up with a delicious bread that has a slight nutty taste from the almond butter. If you can't consume almonds, use cashew butter or sunflower seed butter instead.

7 large eggs

1 cup unsweetened almond butter

½ cup arrowroot starch

½ cup tapioca starch

¼ cup coconut oil

3 tablespoons raw honey

2 teaspoons cream of tartar

1 teaspoon baking soda

½ teaspoon fine sea salt

1. Preheat the oven to 375°F. Line an 8-by-4-inch loaf pan with parchment paper.

2. Using a stand mixer, cream all the ingredients together. Pour the batter into the loaf pan.

3. Bake for 40 to 50 minutes, until a toothpick inserted into the middle comes out dry.

4. Allow the bread to cool in the pan for 10 minutes, then remove from the pan and let cool completely on a cooling rack before slicing.

5. Store the bread in an airtight container at room temperature for up to 2 days, or preslice the bread and store in the freezer for up to 3 months.

Grain-Free TORTILLAS

Yield: 6 tortillas   *Prep time:* 5 minutes   *Cook time:* 12 minutes

These grain-free tortillas are easy to make and taste pretty much identical to traditional flour tortillas, so you can use them in any recipe that normally uses tortillas. Pay careful attention to how long you cook them: overcooking results in hard tortillas rather than soft, pliable ones.

1 cup arrowroot starch

½ cup almond flour

¼ cup tapioca starch

3 tablespoons sifted coconut flour

⅛ teaspoon fine sea salt

½ to ⅔ cup water

1. In a bowl, mix together all the ingredients except for the water. Add ½ cup water and mix with your hands to form a stiff and dense dough. If the dough is not stiff and dense, add up to 2½ tablespoons more water. Separate the dough into 6 balls. Cover the unused dough balls with plastic wrap to prevent them from drying out while forming the tortillas.

2. Take two pieces of parchment paper the size of a large plate. Place one ball of dough on one piece of parchment paper, then top with the other piece of parchment paper. Roll the ball into the thickness of a normal tortilla—less than ⅛ inch, thin but not paper-thin.

3. Heat a 12-inch cast-iron skillet over medium heat.

4. Pull off the top piece of parchment paper. Slide your hand under the parchment paper to pick up the tortilla and place it dough side down in the pan, with the remaining piece of parchment on top. Repeat with a second tortilla.

5. Let the tortillas cook until lightly toasted, 1 to 2 minutes. Remove the parchment paper, flip the tortillas over, and lightly cook the other side for 1 to 2 minutes. Do not overcook or the tortillas will become brittle and won't bend easily.

6. Repeat Steps 2 to 5 with the remaining balls of dough.

7. Consume the tortillas immediately or store in an airtight container at room temperature for up to 2 days. The tortillas can be frozen individually and thawed at room temperature.

Sandwich
BUNS

Yield: 4 or 6 buns, depending on type of mold used   *Prep time:* 5 minutes   *Cook time:* 15 minutes

Almond butter gives these grain-free buns a slight nutty taste, but it's also the reason for the lightness of the buns. The texture is very breadlike. Note that these buns require a mold. You can use mason jar rings for slightly smaller buns or English muffin molds for larger buns.

3 large eggs

½ cup unsweetened almond butter

¼ cup tapioca starch

¼ cup arrowroot starch

¼ cup coconut oil

1 tablespoon raw honey

1 teaspoon cream of tartar

½ teaspoon baking soda

⅛ teaspoon fine sea salt

1 large egg white

1 tablespoon white sesame seeds

Special equipment:

6 wide-mouth mason jar rings or 4 English muffin rings

1. Preheat the oven to 375°F. Line a rimmed baking sheet with parchment paper. Place 6 wide-mouth mason jar rings or 4 English muffin rings on the baking sheet.

2. Using a stand mixer, mix together all the ingredients except the egg white and sesame seeds.

3. Pour the batter into the 6 mason jar rings, filled to just below the rim, or fill 4 English muffin rings halfway. Brush the egg white over the tops of the buns and sprinkle with the sesame seeds.

4. Bake for 15 minutes, or until a toothpick inserted into the middle of a bun comes out dry.

5. Allow the buns to cool, then remove them from the molds. Cut off any excess dough that spilled over the molds during baking.

6. Store the buns in an airtight container at room temperature for up to 2 days, or store in the freezer for up to 3 months.

Grain-Free BAGELS

Yield: 12 bagels   *Prep time:* 5 minutes   *Cook time:* 25 minutes

These bagels are not made in the traditional way, which requires boiling the dough, but the results taste similar and the recipe is less technical. I'm sharing a seasoning for my favorite bagel—the "everything" bagel. Feel free to switch the seasoning for different flavors.

1 cup almond flour

1 cup arrowroot starch

1 cup potato starch

½ cup tapioca starch

¼ cup plus 1 tablespoon sifted coconut flour

1 teaspoon cream of tartar

¾ teaspoon fine sea salt

½ teaspoon baking soda

1 cup water

3 large eggs

¼ cup raw honey

FOR THE 'EVERYTHING' BAGEL SEASONING:

2 teaspoons dried onion flakes

2 teaspoons poppy seeds

2 teaspoons white sesame seeds

1 teaspoon dried minced garlic

1 teaspoon coarse sea salt

Special equipment:

2 (6-cavity) doughnut pans

1. Preheat the oven to 350°F. Grease two 6-cavity doughnut pans.

2. Mix together the almond flour, arrowroot starch, potato starch, tapioca starch, coconut flour, cream of tartar, salt, and baking soda in a medium-sized bowl. In another bowl, mix together the water, eggs, and honey.

3. Pour the wet mixture into the dry ingredients and whisk until combined.

4. In a small bowl, mix together all the seasoning ingredients.

5. Pour the batter evenly into the 12 greased molds, filling the molds almost to the top. Sprinkle the seasoning on each bagel. Bake for 20 to 25 minutes, until a toothpick inserted into the middle of a bagel comes out clean. Allow the bagels to cool completely on a wire rack.

6. Store the bagels in an airtight container at room temperature for up to 2 days, or store in the freezer for up to 3 months.

Sweet Potato
DROP BISCUITS

Yield: 8 biscuits *Prep time:* 20 minutes *Cook time:* 40 minutes

I brag to all my friends that I make the tastiest sweet potato biscuits! The texture of these biscuits is divine. The outside is crispy and the inside is springy and very gluten-like. You're going to love serving these with dinner. Make sure to allow the biscuits to cool before cutting into them. Baked goods made with a large proportion of arrowroot starch can be gooey straight out of the oven, but if you allow them to cool properly, the texture is great.

1 large sweet potato (about ½ pound), peeled and chopped into 1-inch pieces

1 cup arrowroot starch

¼ cup plus 2 tablespoons sifted coconut flour

1 teaspoon cream of tartar

¾ teaspoon baking soda

½ teaspoon fine sea salt

1 tablespoon coconut palm sugar

¼ cup (½ stick) unsalted butter, chilled, cubed

2 large eggs

1 tablespoon unsalted butter, melted, for brushing tops of biscuits

1. Place the sweet potato in a 1½-quart pot and fill with enough water to cover it. Cover and boil for 20 minutes, or until the sweet potato is fork-tender. Drain the water from the pot.

2. Puree with a hand blender, or transfer the sweet potato to a food processor and pulse until smooth.

3. Preheat the oven to 350°F. Line a baking sheet with parchment paper.

4. In the bowl of a stand mixer fitted with the whisk attachment, combine the arrowroot starch, coconut flour, cream of tartar, baking soda, and salt on low speed. Add the sugar and pureed sweet potato and whisk on medium speed until combined. Then add the cubed butter and turn the mixer to its lowest setting; stop mixing when the butter is mixed in but there are still small chunks of butter visible.

5. Add the eggs and continue mixing on the lowest setting until combined.

6. Using two soup spoons, pick up a small amount of the dough, about 2 inches wide, and drop it onto the baking sheet. Drop the rest of the biscuit dough onto the baking sheet in the same way, leaving at least 2 inches between the biscuits.

7. Bake for 40 minutes, or until a toothpick inserted into the middle of a biscuit comes out with a few crumbs. Glaze the tops with the melted butter halfway through baking.

8. These biscuits are best consumed fresh but can be stored in an air-tight container at room temperature for up to 2 days, or store in the freezer for up to 3 months

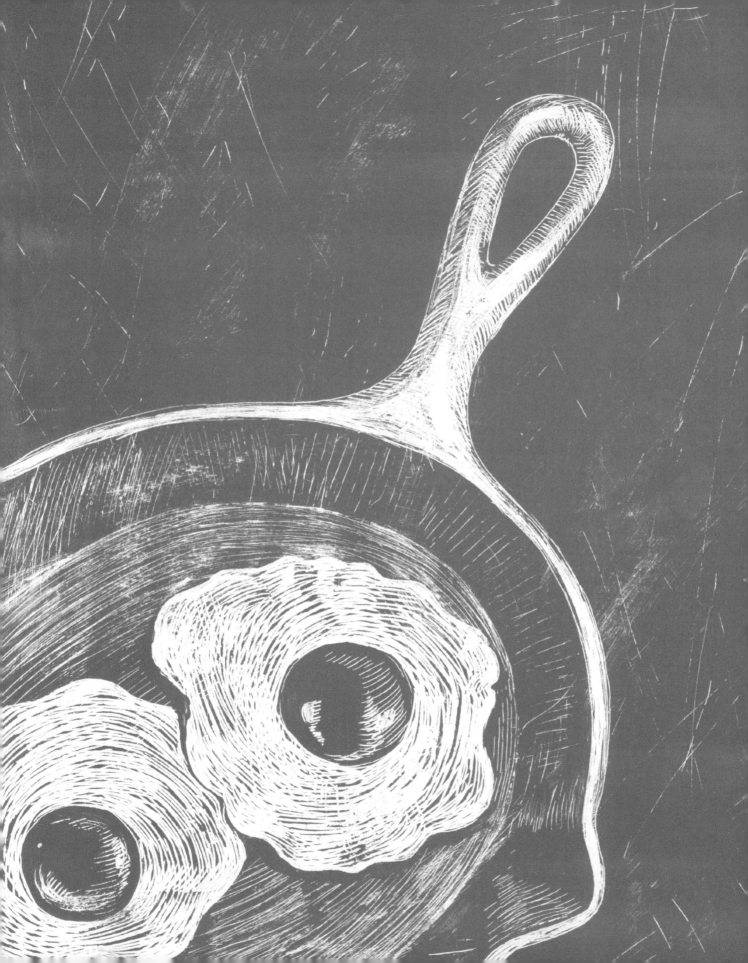

CHAPTER 4

Breakfast FAVORITES

Maple Sage Breakfast
SAUSAGES

Yield: 24 patties (4 to 6 servings)   *Prep time:* 5 minutes   *Cook time:* 20 minutes

In August 2013, I went on a weekend getaway with the Paleo Toronto group to Muskoka, a popular vacation area outside of Toronto referred to as "cottage country." Ever since, I have been craving the maple beef sausages that our host, Shannon, cooked for dinner one night. She told me that a local butcher had made the sausages with grass-fed beef. This is my version, made with pork and sage to add an earthiness reminiscent of the beautiful Muskoka landscape.

2 tablespoons extra-virgin olive oil

½ cup finely chopped onions

2 pounds ground pork

¼ cup plus 2 tablespoons maple syrup

2 teaspoons dry mustard

1 teaspoon fine sea salt

½ teaspoon ground black pepper

½ teaspoon dried rubbed sage

1. In a medium-sized skillet, heat the olive oil over medium heat. Add the onions and sauté until translucent, about 10 minutes. Transfer the onions to a bowl, then wipe out the skillet and set it aside; you will use it to fry the patties.

2. Add the remaining ingredients to the cooked onions and mix thoroughly. Form the sausage mixture into 24 patties, each about 3 inches across.

3. In the same skillet you used to cook the onions, cook the sausages over medium-low heat until they are no longer pink inside and their juices are clear, about 10 minutes, flipping halfway through.

4. Serve immediately, or store in an airtight container in the fridge for up to 5 days or in the freezer for up to 3 months.

Pizza Breakfast
SAUSAGES

Yield: 30 patties (4 to 6 servings)   *Prep time:* 10 minutes   *Cook time:* 30 minutes

Pizza for breakfast? I think so! This is a fun breakfast sausage—a real break from the classic sage-flavored version—that I hope you and your family will love. It's inspired by one of my favorite meals: pizza with all the classic toppings. You can always switch the toppings if you have another favorite pizza flavor. Try Hawaiian!

2 tablespoons extra-virgin olive oil

½ cup finely chopped sweet bell peppers (a variety of green, red, orange, and yellow)

½ cup finely chopped onions

½ cup finely chopped button mushrooms

2 pounds lean ground beef

6 green olives, pitted and finely chopped

2 tablespoons tomato sauce

1 teaspoon fine sea salt

¼ teaspoon ground black pepper

1. Preheat the oven to 400°F. Line a rimmed baking sheet with parchment paper and top with a wire rack.

2. Heat the olive oil in a sauté pan over medium heat. Add the peppers, onions, and mushrooms and sauté until the onions are translucent, about 10 minutes.

3. Transfer the cooked peppers, onions, and mushrooms to a medium-sized bowl and add the beef, olives, tomato sauce, salt, and pepper. Mix thoroughly to combine.

4. Roll the meat mixture into 1-inch balls, then flatten the balls with the palm of your hand. Place the sausages on the baking rack.

5. Bake for 20 minutes, or until the sausages are no longer pink inside.

6. Serve immediately, or store in an airtight container in the fridge for up to 5 days or in the freezer for up to 3 months.

The Original DTW
MEAT BAGEL

Yield: 6 bagels *Prep time:* 10 minutes *Cook time:* 50 minutes

Fans of my blog really dig these meat bagels. They are always sharing with me the different varieties they come up with by changing up the seasonings and switching ground pork for sausage meat. After you try the original recipe, I encourage you to create your own unique meat bagel recipe.

2 tablespoons extra-virgin olive oil

2 small onions, finely diced

2 pounds ground pork

2 large eggs

⅔ cup tomato sauce

1 teaspoon paprika

1 teaspoon fine sea salt

½ teaspoon ground black pepper

Bagel toppings of your choice, such as sliced tomatoes, red onion, or lettuce leaves (optional)

1. Preheat the oven to 400°F. Line a rimmed baking sheet with parchment paper.

2. Heat the olive oil in a 12-inch skillet over medium heat. Add the onions and sauté until translucent, about 10 minutes.

3. In a bowl, mix together the cooked onions, pork, eggs, tomato sauce, paprika, salt, and pepper. Make sure that the spices are evenly distributed.

4. Divide the meat mixture into 6 equal portions. Using your hands, roll a portion into a ball, form a hole in the middle, and flatten slightly to give it the appearance of a bagel.

5. Place the meat bagel on the prepared baking sheet and repeat with the remaining portions of meat.

6. Bake for 40 minutes, or until the juices run clear.

7. Allow the meat bagels to cool to room temperature. Slice the meat bagels just like regular bagels. If desired, fill the meat bagels with toppings such as tomato slices, lettuce, or red onions.

Meat
FRENCH TOAST

Yield: 8 patties (4 servings)   *Prep time:* 5 minutes   *Cook time:* 30 minutes

Well, you know I couldn't just stop at the Original DTW Meat Bagel (page 144). I had to give French toast a meaty twist! Seriously, you have to try this recipe; it's heavenly. I used the flavor profile of Maple Sage Breakfast Sausages (page 140) as my base and then added apples and raisins. After forming it into a mini slice of "bread," you cook it just as you would French toast. I find that the apples and raisins naturally sweeten this meaty French toast enough that I only need to top it with a light drizzle of maple syrup.

4 tablespoons extra-virgin olive oil, divided

1 cup peeled and finely chopped apples (any variety)

1 cup finely chopped onions

1 cup raisins

1 pound ground pork

1 teaspoon ground mustard

½ teaspoon fine sea salt

¼ teaspoon ground black pepper

¼ teaspoon dried rubbed sage

1 large egg

1 teaspoon ground cinnamon

1 teaspoon vanilla extract

Maple syrup, for serving

1. In a large skillet, heat 2 tablespoons of the olive oil over medium heat. Add the apples, onions, and raisins and sauté until the onions are translucent, about 10 minutes.

2. Transfer the onion mixture to a large bowl. Wipe out the skillet and set aside; you will use it to fry the patties. Add the ground pork, mustard, salt, pepper, and sage to the bowl. Mix well enough to evenly distribute the spices.

3. Divide the meat into 8 equal portions. Using your hands, form each portion into a 3-inch square. The patties will be fragile. Lay them on a tray.

4. In the same skillet you used to cook the onions, heat the remaining 2 tablespoons of olive oil over medium-low heat.

5. While the oil is heating up, whisk together the egg, cinnamon, and vanilla in a small bowl. Use a pastry brush to brush the egg mixture over each patty, flip the patties with a spatula, and coat the other side.

6. Place the patties in the skillet. Cook for 5 minutes per side, or until the meat is no longer pink. Serve warm with a drizzle of maple syrup.

Baked
EGGS

Yield: 4 servings   *Prep time:* 5 minutes   *Cook time:* 30 minutes

Baked eggs are for casual weekend mornings. They don't take too long to prepare and bake, and for the little extra effort that goes into making them, they taste divine! The addition of nutritional yeast here creates a slightly cheesy taste. Try these for your next Sunday breakfast.

2 cups chopped spinach

4 slices bacon, cut into ½-inch pieces

½ cup finely chopped onions

2 tablespoons nutritional yeast

8 large eggs

Fine sea salt and ground black pepper

1. Preheat the oven to 375°F.

2. Divide the spinach among 4 personal-sized baking dishes (about 6 inches in length) or four 6-ounce ramekins.

3. In a medium-sized skillet over medium heat, sauté the bacon and onions until the onions are translucent, about 10 minutes.

4. Place the bacon and onions on top of the spinach. Sprinkle the nutritional yeast over the bacon and onions.

5. Crack one egg at a time over the ingredients, using two eggs per serving dish. Sprinkle with salt and pepper. For soft yolks, bake for 15 minutes if using shallow baking dishes or 20 minutes if using ramekins.

6. Serve immediately.

On-the-Go
EGGS

Yield: 8 egg cups *Prep time:* 5 minutes *Cook time:* 35 minutes

There was a stage in my life when I made no time for a nutritious breakfast. Breakfast used to be a fiber bar! I felt that it was more important to make my hair and makeup look fabulous than to fuel my body. If that sounds like you, crush your day by making a large batch of these eggs ahead of time and grab one before you rush out the door. They're easy to eat with your hands.

4 slices thick-cut or 8 slices thin-cut bacon, finely chopped

½ cup finely chopped onions

8 slices ham

8 large eggs

½ cup finely chopped spinach

Fine sea salt and ground black pepper

1. Preheat the oven to 375°F. Grease 8 cups of a 12-well muffin pan.

2. In a medium-sized skillet over medium heat, sauté the bacon and onions until the onions are translucent, about 10 minutes.

3. Fit 1 slice of ham in each of the 8 greased muffin cups. Evenly distribute the spinach, onions, and bacon among the 8 cups. Then crack an egg into each cup. Sprinkle with salt and pepper.

4. Bake for 20 to 25 minutes for fully cooked yolks. Serve hot or cold.

Spicy Brunch
CASSEROLE

Yield: 6 servings   *Prep time:* 10 minutes   *Cook time:* 50 minutes

When I order appetizers at a restaurant, I immediately make laser eye contact with the potato skins. Here, I've turned those crispy, bacon-sprinkled vehicles for deliciousness into a morning dish that you're sure to love! The salsa and jalapeño peppers add a little heat, but nothing sweltering.

8 slices bacon, cut crosswise into ½-inch slices

4 cups ½-inch-cubed white potatoes (4 medium potatoes, unpeeled)

1 medium onion, chopped

¼ red bell pepper, chopped

3 jalapeño peppers, seeds removed, finely chopped

¼ teaspoon fine sea salt, divided

⅛ teaspoon ground black pepper, divided

5 large eggs

¼ cup Salsa (page 68)

1. Preheat the oven to 375°F.

2. In a large cast-iron skillet, cook the bacon over medium heat until crispy, about 5 minutes. Remove the bacon and set on paper towels to drain.

3. Add the potatoes, onion, bell pepper, and jalapeño peppers to the skillet in two batches, seasoning each batch with half of the salt and pepper. Cook over medium heat, covered, until the potatoes are nearly cooked through and are crispy on the outside, about 20 minutes, stirring frequently. The potatoes will not be fully cooked.

4. Put the vegetables and bacon in an 8-inch glass baking dish or 9-by-2-inch pie pan.

5. In a medium-sized bowl, mix together the eggs and salsa. Pour over the ingredients in the baking dish.

6. Bake for 30 minutes, or until the egg is cooked. Let cool for about 10 minutes. When the dish comes out of the oven, there will be a lot of grease, but it will be reabsorbed during the cooling time.

7. Slice into six portions and serve warm.

Grain-Free
WAFFLES

Yield: 6 waffles (3 servings)   *Prep time:* 5 minutes   *Cook time:* 25 minutes

"Eureka!" That's what I exclaimed when I first tasted these waffles. It took some experimenting, but I finally found the right combination of ingredients to create light grain-free waffles that are crisp on the outside and soft on the inside.

1½ cups almond flour

¾ cup arrowroot starch

¼ cup cane sugar

1½ teaspoons cream of tartar

¾ teaspoon baking soda

¾ cup full-fat coconut milk

3 large eggs

½ cup coconut oil, melted but not hot

1 teaspoon fresh lemon juice

Maple syrup, for serving

1. Preheat a waffle iron.

2. Mix together the dry ingredients in a large bowl. In a separate bowl, mix together the wet ingredients.

3. Pour the wet mixture into the dry ingredients and whisk until combined.

4. Grease the waffle iron. Pour the appropriate amount of batter onto the hot waffle iron (refer to the manufacturer's instructions for the proper amount) and cook until the waffle is crisp and brown. Repeat with the remaining batter.

5. Serve immediately with a drizzle of maple syrup.

Coconut Flour
PANCAKES

Yield: Sixteen 3-inch pancakes (4 servings)   *Prep time:* 5 minutes   *Cook time:* 20 minutes

Nothing says "weekend" better than a stack of pancakes! These light, fluffy grain-free pancakes will win over any reluctant family member.

6 large eggs

1 cup full-fat coconut milk

¾ cup plus 2 tablespoons sifted coconut flour

¾ cup tapioca starch

2 tablespoons coconut oil

2 tablespoons maple syrup

2 tablespoons fresh lemon juice

1 teaspoon cream of tartar

½ teaspoon baking soda

½ teaspoon fine sea salt

2 tablespoons ghee (page 56), for the pan

Maple syrup, for serving

Banana slices, for serving (optional)

1. In a large bowl, mix together all the ingredients until smooth. Do not overmix! Overmixing will reduce the effectiveness of the baking soda and cream of tartar, resulting in leaden pancakes.

2. Melt the ghee in a crepe pan or griddle over medium heat. Pour ¼ cup of the batter into the hot pan and spread it around to form a 3-inch pancake, then repeat (so you're cooking two pancakes at once). Flip when the bottom is light brown, about 2 minutes. (These pancakes will not bubble and form holes on the surface like "regular" pancakes do.) Cook for another 1 minute to cook through. Repeat with the remaining batter.

3. Serve immediately with a drizzle of maple syrup and banana slices, if desired.

Yuca
HASH BROWNS

Yield: 4 servings   *Prep time:* 10 minutes   *Cook time:* 50 minutes

This is a nightshade-free hash brown recipe. I have to credit my friend Jennifer Robins, the yuca queen, with introducing me to yuca. Her genius recipes involving yuca set a trend in the Paleo world, leading others to make yuca the star of many dishes. This hash brown recipe was inspired by my friend Aglaee Jacob's use of shredded yuca in her pizza crust. I made her pizza recipe several times, and then it occurred to me that the same technique would make fabulous hash browns!

1 yuca, about 12 inches long, peeled

2 tablespoons extra-virgin olive oil

1 teaspoon fine sea salt, divided

1. Preheat the oven to 375°F. Line a rimmed baking sheet with parchment paper.

2. Shred the yuca with the large holes on a cheese grater.

3. Place the shredded yuca in a medium-sized bowl and pour the olive oil over it. Toss to evenly coat. Dump the yuca out onto the lined baking sheet.

4. Divide the shredded yuca into 12 small piles and shape each pile into a rectangle. Then flatten the piles with your hand to create rectangles that are roughly 2 by 3 inches and ½ inch thick. Sprinkle about half of the salt on top.

5. Bake for 25 minutes. Flip the rectangles and sprinkle the remaining salt on the other side. Bake for another 25 minutes, or until the hash browns are light brown and crispy.

6. Serve immediately.

Snacks & STARTERS

Sweet Potato
NACHO DIP

Yield: About 1 cup   *Prep time:* 10 minutes   *Cook time:* 25 minutes

I love cheese, but I don't digest it well, so traditional nacho cheese dip is not an option for me. This recipe is my alternative to a dairy-based nacho dip. The pureed sweet potato is amazingly creamy and dippable. I assure you, it does not taste like mashed sweet potatoes; it tastes like an addictive nacho-flavored dip that I can't stop scooping with cassava chips.

1 large sweet potato (¾ to 1 pound), peeled and coarsely chopped

½ cup nutritional yeast

¼ cup plus 2 tablespoons extra-virgin olive oil

1 teaspoon onion powder

1 teaspoon red pepper flakes

1 teaspoon fine sea salt

½ teaspoon paprika

¼ teaspoon ground cumin

Pinch of chili powder

Crudités or chips of choice, for serving

1. Place the chopped sweet potato in a 1½-quart pot and fill with enough water to cover.

2. Cover and boil for 20 minutes, or until the sweet potato is fork-tender. Drain the water from the pot, leaving the potato in the pot.

3. Add the nutritional yeast, olive oil, onion powder, red pepper flakes, salt, paprika, cumin, and chili powder to the pot. Puree with a hand blender, or transfer the ingredients to a food processor and pulse until smooth.

4. Transfer the dip to a bowl and serve immediately with your favorite veggies or chips.

Apple Butter
CHICKEN LIVER PÂTÉ

Yield: About 4 cups *Prep time:* 5 minutes *Cook time:* 15 minutes

If you don't like liver, this is the easiest way to consume it. This pâté is sweet instead of savory. It has a very creamy texture that you will love spreading on crackers or apple slices. The fat seal on top acts as a preservative, so the pâté will keep for a couple of weeks in the fridge. I often freeze my pâté in individual servings and thaw it in the fridge before serving.

¼ cup (½ stick) plus 2 tablespoons unsalted butter, cubed, divided

½ cup finely diced onions

1 pound chicken livers

1 teaspoon fine sea salt

½ teaspoon ground black pepper

¼ cup Apple Butter (page 70)

¼ cup ghee (page 56), melted (optional)

Crudités or crackers of choice, for serving

1. In a large skillet, heat 2 tablespoons of the butter over medium heat. Add the onion to the hot pan and cook, stirring frequently, until soft, about 10 minutes. Place the cooked onion in a bowl.

2. Place the chicken livers in the same skillet and cook for 2 minutes per side. You just need to brown them. The livers will be pink inside, which is what you want; this gives the pâté a smooth texture.

3. Place the onions, livers, salt, pepper, apple butter, and the remaining ¼ cup of butter in a food processor and pulse until smooth.

4. Pour the pâté into two 16-ounce jars. If not consuming the pâté the same day, you can seal it by pouring the melted ghee over the top of the pâté.

5. Refrigerate for at least an hour or, better yet, let the flavors develop further by refrigerating overnight.

6. Serve with crackers. When serving pâté that has been sealed with ghee, you can either eat the ghee or discard it.

7. The pâté will last for 2 weeks in the refrigerator with the ghee seal.

Dates Stuffed with
COCONUT BUTTER

Yield: 12 stuffed dates   *Prep time:* 10 minutes

This is an extremely easy snack to prepare. It's made with two ingredients, dates and coconut butter, and it doesn't require any cooking. Coconut butter, made from the meat of the coconut, has a natural sweetness to it. You'll find yourself eating it by the spoonful if you like coconut. Note that although it's called "butter," coconut butter is less creamy than most butters.

---

12 Medjool dates

¾ cup coconut butter

1. Slice a date open lengthwise (don't halve the date, though). Pick out the pit and discard.

2. Scoop out about 1 tablespoon of coconut butter and mold it with your hands to the shape of the date, but slightly smaller. Then insert it into the date. Close the date back up and use your hands to shape the coconut butter into the date.

3. Repeat this process with the remaining dates and coconut butter.

4. Serve immediately or store at room temperature for up to a week.

Plantain CHIPS

Yield: 2 cups   *Prep time:* 5 minutes   *Cook time:* 30 minutes

Plantain chips are addicting, especially when sprinkled with salt. I've found that baking them at a lower temperature prevents burning. When purchasing plantains for making chips, look for ones that are yellow with black spots. You can also buy green plantains and allow them to ripen on your kitchen counter, as you would with green bananas.

2 ripe plantains

½ cup coconut oil, melted

Fine sea salt

1. Preheat the oven to 300°F. Line 2 rimmed baking sheets with parchment paper.

2. Peel the plantains, then, using a mandoline or knife, slice thinly into rounds. Make sure that the slices are about ⅛ inch thick.

3. Place the plantain slices in a mixing bowl. Add the coconut oil and mix until the slices are coated. Arrange the slices on the baking sheets, making sure to not overlap them.

4. Bake for 30 minutes, or until the edges are brown. The chips in the middle might require additional baking time.

5. Transfer the chips to a bowl, sprinkle with salt, and toss to mix. Serve immediately or store cooled chips in an airtight container for up to 2 days.

BBQ Kale
CHIPS

Yield: About 2 cups   *Prep time:* 5 minutes   *Cook time:* 15 minutes

My favorite potato chip flavor is barbecue, so it was only natural that I'd want to make my own naturally flavored version using kale instead of potatoes! When you prepare the kale, make sure to thoroughly wash and then thoroughly dry it. The washing step is important because kale from a farmers' market can have quite a bit of dirt clinging to the leaves. The drying step is key because it affects the crispiness of the kale chips; damp kale equals soggy chips.

FOR THE BBQ SPICE MIX (MAKES 1 ABOUT TABLESPOON):

1 teaspoon coconut palm sugar
½ teaspoon paprika
½ teaspoon fine sea salt
¼ teaspoon garlic powder
¼ teaspoon onion powder
¼ teaspoon ground black pepper
Pinch of cayenne pepper
2 drops of natural liquid smoke

1 bunch kale
2 tablespoons extra-virgin olive oil

1. Preheat the oven to 350°F. Line 2 rimmed baking sheets with parchment paper.

2. Combine all the spice mix ingredients in a small bowl.

3. Wash and thoroughly dry the kale. Using your hands or a knife, separate the stems from the leaves and discard the stems, which do not bake well. Rip or cut the leaves into chip-sized pieces.

4. Place the kale in a large bowl. Pour the olive oil over the kale and toss to coat. Sprinkle the spice mixture over the kale and toss again.

5. Place the kale on the baking sheets; do not overcrowd. Overcrowding will result in soggy chips. Bake for 10 to 15 minutes. The more kale on the baking sheets, the longer it takes for the chips to bake.

6. After 10 minutes of baking, begin to watch the leaves carefully. If they burn, they will taste bitter. When the chips are crispy, they are done. If some leaves are still soft, just put them back in the oven for a little longer.

7. Consume the chips immediately.

Spicy Nori CHIPS

Yield: About 1 cup   *Prep time:* 5 minutes   *Cook time:* 7 minutes

Seaweed isn't just for sushi! It makes excellent chips, and when you season it with Sriracha sauce and coconut aminos, you get spicy, salty chips that don't taste fishy. You can find nori sheets in the international aisle of your supermarket. Nori sheets crisp up very fast, so don't leave these in the oven too long. I find it easier to tear them into chip-sized pieces after I bake them.

3 nori sheets

1 tablespoon extra-virgin olive oil

1 teaspoon Sriracha sauce, homemade (page 96) or store-bought

1 teaspoon coconut aminos

Fine sea salt

1. Preheat the oven to 300°F. Line a baking sheet with parchment paper.

2. Cut the nori sheets in half.

3. In a small bowl, mix together the olive oil, Sriracha, and coconut aminos. Lightly brush the sauce on both sides of the nori. Sprinkle one side with salt.

4. Bake for 7 minutes, or until the nori is crisp.

5. Rip or cut into chip-sized pieces and serve immediately.

Artichoke with
BACON SPINACH DIP

Yield: 4 servings   *Prep time:* 15 minutes   *Cook time:* 45 minutes

While I was working on my second cookbook, an e-book titled *The Grain-Free Snacker*, this was my favorite recipe. Artichoke leaves make great dippers. For those of you who have never eaten a fresh artichoke, here's a tutorial: First, remove a leaf and, holding it by its tip, dip the base into the bacon spinach dip. Then put the wide part in your mouth, bite down, and pull the leaf through your teeth to remove the soft portion; discard the fibrous leaf.

FOR THE DIP:

1 recipe Homemade Aioli (page 64)

5 cloves garlic, finely chopped

½ cup finely chopped fresh spinach

¼ cup chopped onions

2 slices bacon, chopped and cooked

2 large artichokes

1 teaspoon fine sea salt

1. Make the dip: Combine the aioli with the garlic, spinach, onions, and bacon in a medium-sized bowl. Store in the fridge while you prepare the artichoke.

2. Trim the tips off the artichokes.

3. In a 3-quart pot, bring ½ inch of water and the salt to a boil.

4. Place the artichokes in the boiling water and cover the pot with a lid. Reduce the heat to a simmer and steam for 40 minutes. The artichokes are done when you can easily pull off a leaf.

5. To serve, pull the leaves off the artichokes and place them on a plate. Use the leaves to scoop the dip.

6. Store leftover dip in the fridge for up to 2 days.

Sun-Dried Tomato & Basil
HUMMUS

Yield: 1 cup *Prep time:* 10 minutes *Cook time:* 15 minutes

This is a sneaky way to include extra vegetables in your diet. Cauliflower replaces traditional chickpeas to make an amazing base for hummus. You would never know that it's cauliflower!

¼ head cauliflower (about 7 ounces), chopped

¼ cup chopped sun-dried tomatoes, plus more for garnish

3 tablespoons tahini

3 tablespoons fresh lemon juice

2 cloves garlic, chopped

2 tablespoons chopped fresh basil, plus more for garnish

¼ teaspoon fine sea salt

Extra-virgin olive oil, for drizzling

Crudités, for serving

1. Place the chopped cauliflower in a 1-quart pot and add enough water to cover it. Bring to a boil and cook for 10 minutes, or until the cauliflower is fork-tender.

2. Drain the cauliflower and return it to the pot. Add the sun-dried tomatoes, tahini, lemon juice, garlic, basil, and salt. Puree with a hand blender, or transfer the ingredients to a food processor and pulse until smooth.

3. Serve warm with a drizzle of olive oil and sprinkle of chopped sun-dried tomatoes and basil, or chill in the refrigerator and garnish before serving.

4. Serve with cut-up vegetables.

Onion FRIES

Yield: 4 servings *Prep time:* 10 minutes *Cook time:* 12 minutes

This is a fun party snack. The coating is thin and crispy, and the fried onion wedges are the perfect dippers for your favorite dipping sauce!

2 cups coconut oil (see Note)

2 large onions

½ cup arrowroot starch

½ teaspoon garlic powder

½ teaspoon paprika

½ teaspoon fine sea salt

¼ teaspoon cayenne pepper

⅛ teaspoon ground black pepper

2 large egg whites

1 recipe Smoky Chipotle Aioli (page 66), for serving

1. In a 4-quart pot or deep fryer, heat the coconut oil to 350°F.

2. Cut off the tops (not the root ends) of the onions, then peel and cut into ½-inch wedges. Separate all the wedges and set aside.

3. Place the arrowroot starch, garlic powder, paprika, salt, cayenne, and black pepper in a large bowl.

4. In another large bowl, whisk the egg whites until frothy. Add the flour mixture and whisk to combine.

5. Dip all the onion pieces in the batter, using a spoon to make sure that all the pieces are coated.

6. When the oil reaches 350°F, gently lower small batches of the coated onion pieces into the oil and fry for about 2 minutes, or until golden brown.

7. Using a slotted spoon, remove the onion fries from the oil and place on a paper towel to soak up the excess oil. Repeat with the rest of the onion pieces.

8. Serve warm with Smoky Chipotle Aioli for dipping.

Note: *I prefer to use coconut oil for frying because it is a natural fat. It will take on a golden hue after you use it. After deep-frying with coconut oil, strain the oil through a fine-mesh sieve and store it in the fridge for future use. You can reuse coconut oil for frying several times.*

Salted Mexican
CHOCOLATE CLUSTERS

Yield: 20 clusters *Prep time:* 5 minutes *Cook time:* 7 minutes, plus 30 minutes to freeze

When you're craving a chocolaty snack, try these clusters. They're fun to eat, and you can make them in the blink of an eye to get your chocolate fix. When trying various finishing salts for these chocolates, I discovered that I liked the mild taste of kosher salt best (sea salt crystals were just too intensely salty for me). You may use any finishing salt you like, though.

1¼ cups semi-sweet chocolate chips

1 cup raw almonds

1 cup raisins

1 teaspoon chipotle powder

1 teaspoon ground cinnamon

½ teaspoon kosher salt, plus more for garnish

1. Line a rimmed baking sheet with parchment or wax paper.

2. Place the chocolate chips in a heavy-bottomed 1-quart pot over low heat. Stir continuously until the chocolate chips have melted. Alternatively, you can place the chocolate chips in a microwave-safe bowl and heat in 30-second intervals, stirring between intervals, until melted.

3. Place the melted chocolate and the rest of the ingredients in a bowl and mix to combine.

4. Using a large spoon, scoop up some of the mixture and place it on the lined baking sheet. Use your fingers to form it into a round shape. Repeat with the rest of the mixture until you have 20 round clusters. Lightly sprinkle salt on each cluster. Put the baking sheet in the freezer until the clusters are firm, about 30 minutes.

5. Store the clusters in the fridge for up to 2 weeks.

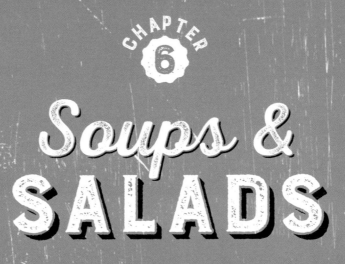

CHAPTER 6

Soups & SALADS

Hearty Beef
STEW

Yield: 4 servings *Prep time:* 10 minutes *Cook time:* 8 hours

I hated stew for most of my life. To me, it was unfathomable to eat something covered in gravy. I was that kid (and I'm still very much like this) who could not handle my food touching, let alone being covered in, a sauce. Then, a few years ago, a friend served me gluten-free stew, and I thought to myself, "Oh wow, why have I been avoiding this all my life?!" Since then I've made beef bourguignonne and other stews countless times. This is my version of a simple hearty beef stew that you can enjoy on cold winter days.

4 slices bacon, chopped

1½ pounds stewing beef

2 carrots, peeled and chopped

2 large onions, chopped

1 stalk celery, chopped

6 cups Beef Bone Broth (page 77)

4 sweet potatoes, peeled and cut into 1-inch chunks

½ cup tomato paste

4 bay leaves

1 tablespoon chopped fresh rosemary leaves

2 teaspoons chopped fresh thyme leaves

1 teaspoon fine sea salt, plus more to season the beef

1 teaspoon ground black pepper, plus more to season the beef

2 tablespoons arrowroot starch, plus more if needed

1. In a 12-inch skillet, cook the bacon over medium heat, then transfer it to an 8-quart slow cooker. Leave the bacon fat in the pan.

2. Season the beef with salt and pepper and brown it in the skillet with the bacon fat. Once browned on all sides, place it in the slow cooker.

3. In the same skillet, sauté the carrots, onions, and celery until the onions are soft, about 10 minutes, then transfer them to the slow cooker.

4. Add the bone broth, sweet potatoes, tomato paste, herbs, 1 teaspoon salt, and 1 teaspoon pepper to the slow cooker and stir to combine. Turn the heat to high to bring to a boil, then reduce to low and cook for 8 hours, or until the meat is fork-tender.

5. To thicken the gravy, scoop 1 cup of the sauce out of the slow cooker and pour it in a small mixing bowl. Add the arrowroot starch and whisk until combined. Pour the mixture back into the slow cooker and stir. Continue adding arrowroot 1 tablespoon at a time, whisking after each addition, until it reaches the desired thickness.

6. Remove the bay leaves. Consume immediately or, for optimal flavor, serve the next day.

Dairy-Free
SHRIMP BISQUE

Yield: 4 servings *Prep time:* 10 minutes *Cook time:* 40 minutes

For the longest time, even though I made bone broth all the time, I was intimidated by the thought of making soup from scratch. It was my friend Rachael of the blog *Meatified* who showed me that it's as easy as picking a protein, a trio of vegetables, and a base. In this case, I took a creamy coconut base and pureed everything to create a mind-blowingly amazing soup. This was my first attempt at soup many years ago and remains my favorite.

1 tablespoon ghee (page 56)

12 large shrimp, deveined, shells on

1 cup chopped carrots

1 cup chopped celery

1 cup chopped onions

1 (6-ounce) can tomato paste

1 cup coconut cream (see page 33)

4 cups Chicken Bone Broth (page 77)

1 teaspoon fine sea salt

½ teaspoon ground black pepper

4 sprigs flat-leaf parsley, for garnish (optional)

1. Heat the ghee in a 6-quart pot over medium heat. Add the shrimp and sauté until pink. Remove the shrimp and place the carrots, celery, and onions in the pot. Sauté the vegetables until they are soft, about 10 minutes.

2. Peel the shells off the shrimp and return the shrimp to the pot with the vegetables. Add the tomato paste and coconut cream.

3. Puree with a hand blender, or transfer the ingredients to a food processor and pulse until smooth, then return the puree to the pot.

4. Add the bone broth and simmer over medium heat for 30 minutes to achieve a creamy thickness. Add the salt and pepper, taste for seasoning, and add more if needed.

5. Pour into four serving bowls and garnish with parsley, if desired.

Roasted Butternut Squash
SOUP

Yield: 4 servings   *Prep time:* 15 minutes   *Cook time:* 1 hour 20 minutes

This creamy soup is good for your body because, like all the soups in this chapter, it is packed with bone broth, which is incredibly soothing for your intestinal tract. Roasted butternut squash is a tasty way to consume plenty of bone broth.

3 cups 1-inch-cubed butternut squash (about 2 pounds butternut squash)

1 large onion, quartered

3 tablespoons ghee (page 56), melted, divided

2 teaspoons fine sea salt, divided

1 teaspoon ground black pepper, divided

¼ red bell pepper, chopped

4 cloves garlic, chopped

4 cups Chicken Bone Broth (page 77), divided

Fresh cilantro leaves, for garnish (optional)

1. Preheat the oven to 425°F. Line a rimmed baking sheet with parchment paper.

2. Place the butternut squash and onion on the prepared baking sheet. Drizzle 2 tablespoons of the ghee all over them and sprinkle with 1 teaspoon of the salt and ½ teaspoon of the pepper. Roast for 40 minutes, flipping halfway through.

3. In a 6-quart pot, heat the remaining 1 tablespoon of ghee, then sauté the bell pepper and garlic until the pepper is soft.

4. Add the roasted butternut squash and onion and 2 cups of the bone broth to the pot. Use a hand blender to puree until smooth, or puree in a food processor in batches and then return the puree to the pot. Add the remaining 2 cups of broth, 1 teaspoon of salt, and ½ teaspoon of pepper.

5. Simmer over medium heat, stirring occasionally, for 30 minutes to achieve a creamy thickness. Add more salt and pepper to taste, if needed. Garnish each bowl of soup with a few cilantro leaves, if desired.

Roasted Garlic &
SWEET RED PEPPER SOUP

Yield: 4 servings   *Prep time:* 10 minutes   *Cook time:* 1 hour 10 minutes

Roasting the vegetables takes this soup to the next level—the red bell peppers end up with such a depth of flavor. I also love the creaminess that is created without the use of heavy cream.

---

6 large red bell peppers, seeded and quartered

2 large onions, quartered

4 cloves garlic, peeled

2 tablespoons ghee (page 56), melted

1 (6-ounce) can tomato paste

2 tablespoons chopped fresh basil

1 tablespoon chopped fresh thyme

4 cups Chicken Bone Broth (page 77), divided

1 teaspoon fine sea salt, plus more for seasoning the vegetables

½ teaspoon ground black pepper, plus more for seasoning the vegetables

1. Preheat the oven to 425°F. Line a rimmed baking sheet with parchment paper.

2. Arrange the bell peppers, onions, and garlic on the prepared baking sheet. Drizzle the ghee all over them and sprinkle generously with salt and pepper. Roast the vegetables until they are brown and tender, turning the peppers and onions occasionally, about 40 minutes.

3. Place the roasted vegetables in a large pot. Add the tomato paste, basil, thyme, and 2 cups of the bone broth. Use a hand blender to puree until smooth, or puree in a food processor in batches and then return the puree to the pot. Add the remaining 2 cups of broth, the salt, and the pepper and stir.

4. Simmer over medium heat, stirring occasionally, for 30 minutes to achieve a creamy thickness. Add more salt and pepper to taste, if needed. Serve immediately.

Roasted Tomato & Basil
SOUP

Yield: 4 servings   *Prep time:* 10 minutes   *Cook time:* 1 hour 40 minutes

Tomato soup is something I only appreciated once I grew up. My dad used to eat tomato soup all the time when I was a kid, and I just didn't understand why anyone would eat soup, let alone a bowl of pureed tomatoes. I was a kid who lived on chicken. But as an adult, I found myself with too many tomatoes that I needed to use up and decided to try tomato soup. Here's my grown-up, nutritious and delicious version of tomato soup.

12 Roma tomatoes, halved lengthwise

4 tablespoons ghee (page 56), melted, divided

1 large onion, diced

4 cloves garlic, chopped

1 cup coconut cream (see page 33)

1 (6-ounce) can tomato paste

2 tablespoons chopped fresh basil leaves

1 teaspoon raw apple cider vinegar

4 cups Chicken Bone Broth (page 77), divided

1 teaspoon fine sea salt, plus more for seasoning the tomatoes

½ teaspoon ground black pepper, plus more for seasoning the tomatoes

1. Preheat the oven to 425°F. Line a rimmed baking sheet with parchment paper.

2. Arrange the tomatoes on the prepared baking sheet and drizzle 3 tablespoons of the ghee all over them, then sprinkle generously with salt and pepper. Roast for 1 hour.

3. Heat the remaining 1 tablespoon of ghee in a 6-quart pot over medium heat. Add the onion and sauté for 5 minutes, then add the garlic and sauté for an additional 5 minutes.

4. Add the roasted tomatoes, coconut cream, tomato paste, dried basil, vinegar, and 2 cups of the bone broth. Use a hand blender to puree until smooth, or puree in a food processor in batches and then return the puree to the pot. Add the remaining 2 cups of broth, the salt, and the pepper and stir.

5. Simmer over medium heat, stirring occasionally, for 30 minutes to achieve a creamy thickness. Add more salt and pepper to taste, if needed. Serve immediately.

Chicken Enchilada
SOUP

Yield: 4 servings   *Prep time:* 20 minutes   *Cook time:* 1 hour

This soup is inspired by my love of chicken, cilantro, and Mexican cuisine. If you are a cilantro hater, please walk away! We can't be friends anymore. The cilantro garnish completes this dish, so please use only fresh cilantro and add it when you're ready to sit down and take your first slurp of this epic soup that is going to complete your life.

2 tablespoons extra-virgin olive oil

2 bone-in chicken breasts (about 1 pound)

½ cup diced green bell peppers

½ cup diced yellow bell peppers

½ cup diced red bell peppers

¼ jalapeño pepper, diced and seeded

½ cup diced onions

2 cloves garlic, chopped

4 cups Chicken Bone Broth (page 77)

1 cup tomato sauce

1 large sweet potato, peeled and chopped into 1-inch pieces

1 teaspoon ground cumin

1 teaspoon red pepper flakes

1 teaspoon fine sea salt, plus more for seasoning the chicken

½ teaspoon ground black pepper, plus more for seasoning the chicken

¼ cup chopped fresh cilantro

1. In a 6-quart pot, heat the olive oil over medium-high heat. Season the chicken with salt and pepper. Brown the chicken for 3 minutes per side, then remove it from the pot and set aside.

2. To the pot, add the bell peppers, jalapeño pepper, onions, and garlic and sauté until the onions are soft, about 10 minutes. Return the chicken to the pot and add the bone broth, tomato sauce, sweet potato, cumin, red pepper flakes, salt, and pepper.

3. Simmer uncovered over medium heat, stirring occasionally, for 40 minutes. Remove the chicken, shred it with two forks, and set aside. Discard the bones and skin.

4. Use a hand blender to puree the soup until smooth, or puree in a food processor in batches and then return the puree to the pot. Add the shredded chicken and more salt and pepper to taste, if needed.

5. Garnish with the cilantro and serve immediately.

Tomato Basil
SALAD

Yield: 4 servings   *Prep time:* 10 minutes

This simple salad celebrates those cute mini tomatoes that you can buy at the farmers' market. I always buy them because their cuteness draws me in, but I never really had a use for them until I made this salad. Any miniature tomato variety will work in this recipe, including cherry and mini heirloom tomatoes.

½ cup peeled and sliced cucumbers

2 cups grape tomatoes, halved

½ cup diced red onions

2 tablespoons chopped fresh basil

FOR THE DRESSING:

¼ cup extra-light virgin olive oil

2 tablespoons balsamic vinegar

⅛ teaspoon fine sea salt

Pinch of ground black pepper

1. Slice the cucumber rounds into quarters.

2. Place the cucumbers, tomatoes, onions, and basil in a large mixing bowl.

3. In a small bowl, whisk together the olive oil, balsamic vinegar, salt, and pepper. Pour the dressing over the salad and toss to coat.

4. Serve immediately.

BLT Wedge
SALAD

Yield: 4 servings   *Prep time:* 15 minutes

Wedge salads are a lot of fun. They're basically regular salads that are presented in a creative way. Most wedge salads use iceberg lettuce, but I prefer the softness of butter lettuce for this recipe. Don't forget to serve this salad with a knife.

1 head Boston or butter lettuce, washed and cut through the core into 4 wedges

½ cup Dairy-Free Creamy Caesar Dressing (page 58)

4 slices bacon, cooked

½ tomato, chopped

¼ cup chopped red onions

1. Place the lettuce wedges on a large platter or four individual salad plates. Spoon 2 tablespoons of the dressing over each wedge.

2. Chop the bacon and sprinkle it over the wedges. Sprinkle the chopped tomato and onions on top.

3. Serve immediately.

Kale Citrus
SALAD

Yield: 4 servings *Prep time:* 15 minutes

Massaged kale salads are delicious. This one packs a punch of citrus flavor, and the almonds add a satisfying crunch. The change in texture that occurs when you take the time to massage the kale is incredible. I wouldn't want to eat it any other way.

2 cups stemmed and chopped kale (about ½ bunch)

¼ cup Spicy Citrus Salad Dressing (page 62)

2 pink or red grapefruits

½ cup sliced almonds

¼ red onion, thinly sliced

1. Place the kale in a large mixing bowl. Pour the dressing all over the kale and toss to coat. Using clean hands, massage the kale until the dressing begins to break down the cellulose, softening the kale. This takes about 5 minutes.

2. Use a paring knife to slice off the top and bottom of each grapefruit. Remove all the peel and pith, including the exposed membranes of the segments. Use the knife to remove each individual segment, leaving the membranes behind. Place the segments in the mixing bowl with the kale.

3. Add the almonds and red onion to the mixing bowl. Toss and serve immediately.

Apple Walnut
SALAD

Yield: 4 servings   *Prep time:* 15 minutes

I want to be honest: I designed this salad to be a vehicle for a maple syrup–based salad dressing. I adore maple syrup. When you make this salad, do not, under any circumstances, even if the world is ending and zombies are taking over and all you can find is fake maple syrup, use fake maple syrup, or you'll make someone in Canada cry.

6 cups mixed salad greens

8 slices bacon, cooked and chopped

1 medium green apple (any variety), cored and cut into ¼-inch-wide slices

½ cup unsweetened dried cranberries

½ cup raw walnut pieces

Up to ¾ cup Maple Balsamic Salad Dressing (page 60)

1. Place the greens, bacon, apple slices, cranberries, walnuts, and ½ cup of the dressing in a large bowl and toss to coat. If you feel that you need more dressing, add up to ¼ cup more in 1-tablespoon increments.

2. Serve immediately.

Warm Dandelion
PEAR SALAD

Yield: 4 servings   *Prep time:* 10 minutes   *Cook time:* 2 minutes

Dandelion greens are extremely healthy for you and help your body detox. Unfortunately, they're also naturally bitter-tasting. The sweetness of the pear and raisins in this salad balance out the bitterness and make it delicious. I love eating this salad with chicken.

2 tablespoons extra-virgin olive oil

½ pound dandelion greens, stemmed and halved

1 ripe pear (any variety), peeled and sliced into ½-inch wedges

¼ cup golden or regular raisins

¼ cup pine nuts

¼ cup balsamic vinegar

1. Heat the olive oil in a large skillet over medium heat. Add all the ingredients except the balsamic vinegar to the skillet. Cook, stirring frequently, until the dandelion greens are slightly wilted, about 2 minutes.

2. Pour the balsamic vinegar over the wilted greens and toss. Serve immediately.

MAIN MEALS

Salmon with
MANGO SALSA

Yield: 4 servings   *Prep time:* 15 minutes   *Cook time:* 20 minutes

Fruit salsas always pair well with fish such as salmon, which is a simple fish that's easy for a novice cook to prepare: just season it with salt and pepper and then cook it on medium heat, flipping once. It's easy to tell when salmon is fully cooked because it flakes. I also like salmon because you can always find it sold wild at your grocery store.

FOR THE SALSA:

2 ripe mangoes, peeled and cut into ½-inch cubes

½ cup chopped red onions

½ cup chopped fresh cilantro

Juice of 2 limes

FOR THE SALMON:

4 (5- to 6-ounce) skinless salmon fillets

Fine sea salt and ground black pepper

2 tablespoons extra-virgin olive oil

1. Make the salsa: Combine the mangoes, onions, and cilantro in a small bowl. Pour the lime juice over it and toss.

2. Season the fish with salt and pepper. Heat the olive oil in a 12-inch skillet over medium heat. Place two salmon fillets presentation side (the side you want to display when you serve it) down in the hot pan. Cook until the bottom begins to brown, about 5 minutes. Flip and cook until the salmon is flaky and the flesh is opaque, about 5 minutes.

3. Repeat with the remaining two fillets. Serve each salmon fillet with a spoonful of salsa on top.

Curry Shrimp
DISH

Yield: 4 servings *Prep time:* 10 minutes *Cook time:* 7 minutes, plus 15 minutes for the cauliflower rice

I never got into eating Thai food until I started eating Paleo. On my first night at the Ancestral Health Symposium, I was waiting for my roommate, Lindsay, to arrive before getting dinner. By the time her flight got in, we were starving. She suggested that we order Thai and skip the rice. I had never had Thai food before, and it was amazing! Staying with Lindsay that weekend also changed the course of my blog. I told her that I wanted to write my first cookbook and offer it as an e-book, but I lacked the confidence to follow through. Lindsay built up my confidence, and six months later my first cookbook, *Indulge*, was ready. Here's the dish that started it all.

2 tablespoons extra-virgin olive oil

2 cups chopped broccoli

1 medium onion, chopped

1 large red bell pepper, chopped

1 tablespoon minced fresh ginger

2 cups coconut cream (see page 33)

2 tablespoons Thai red curry paste

1 tablespoon fish sauce

20 large shrimp, peeled and deveined

1 recipe Cauliflower Rice (page 272), for serving

1. Heat the olive oil in a 12-inch skillet over medium-high heat. Add the broccoli, onion, bell pepper, and ginger and sauté for 3 minutes.

2. Pour in the coconut cream, curry paste, and fish sauce and stir to blend in the curry paste. Add the shrimp and cook until opaque, about 3 minutes.

3. Serve over cauliflower rice.

Spicy Fish Cakes with
DIPPING SAUCE

Yield: 4 servings   *Prep time:* 10 minutes   *Cook time:* 20 minutes

I'm always looking for more ways to eat healthy fish. These piquant fish cakes are a grown-up version of bland fish sticks: a crunchy exterior contrasts with a moist and tender interior, with a hint of spiciness.

½ cup almond flour

2 (6-ounce) cans salmon, drained

2 large eggs

½ cup chopped onions

¼ cup diced red bell peppers

2½ tablespoons Homemade Aioli (page 64) or mayonnaise

2 tablespoons Dijon mustard

1 tablespoon dried parsley

½ teaspoon Sriracha sauce, homemade (page 96) or store-bought

¼ teaspoon fine sea salt

1 tablespoon chopped fresh flat-leaf parsley, for garnish (optional)

1 recipe Extra-Garlicky Sriracha Aioli (page 66), for serving

1. Preheat the oven to 350°F. Line a rimmed baking sheet with parchment paper.

2. Place the almond flour in a small bowl.

3. Place the rest of the ingredients in a food processor and pulse until well combined. Scoop the mixture into 10 balls.

4. Dip the fish cakes into the bowl of almond flour, evenly coating both sides. Place the flour-coated cakes on the lined baking sheet.

5. Bake for 20 minutes, flipping the cakes once halfway through.

6. Garnish with chopped fresh parsley, if desired, and serve with Extra-Garlicky Sriracha Aioli.

Mussels with
BUTTER BROTH

Yield: 4 servings   *Prep time:* 15 minutes   *Cook time:* 25 minutes

There is nothing more indulgent than smooth, delicious butter broth. What is butter broth, you might ask? I start with chicken bone broth, infuse it with garlic and onions (perfect companions for any seafood), and then finish by adding butter, which makes the broth velvety and rich. After enjoying the mussels, make sure to eat the broth by the spoonful. If you eat just the mussels, you'll miss out on half of the pleasure that this dish has to offer.

3 pounds fresh mussels

2 tablespoons unsalted butter plus 5 tablespoons unsalted butter, chilled, diced

½ medium onion, chopped

4 cloves garlic, chopped

2 cups Chicken Bone Broth (page 77)

1 tablespoon raw apple cider vinegar

1 teaspoon Dijon mustard

¼ cup chopped fresh flat-leaf parsley, for garnish

1. Rinse the mussels under cold water. Scrub the shells and pull any tough fibers (called the beard) off of the mussels.

2. Heat the 2 tablespoons of butter in a 6-quart stockpot over medium heat. Add the onion and garlic and sauté until the onion is translucent, about 10 minutes.

3. Pour in the bone broth and vinegar, then add the mustard. Bring to a simmer.

4. Add the mussels and cook, covered, until all the mussels open, about 6 minutes. Discard any unopened mussels.

5. Use a slotted spoon to scoop the mussels into four serving bowls.

6. Reduce the heat under the pot to the lowest setting to keep the broth warm (do not allow it to simmer) and gradually add the 5 tablespoons of chilled, diced butter, whisking constantly; the broth will thicken slightly and take on a beautiful sheen. Immediately pour over the mussels and garnish with parsley.

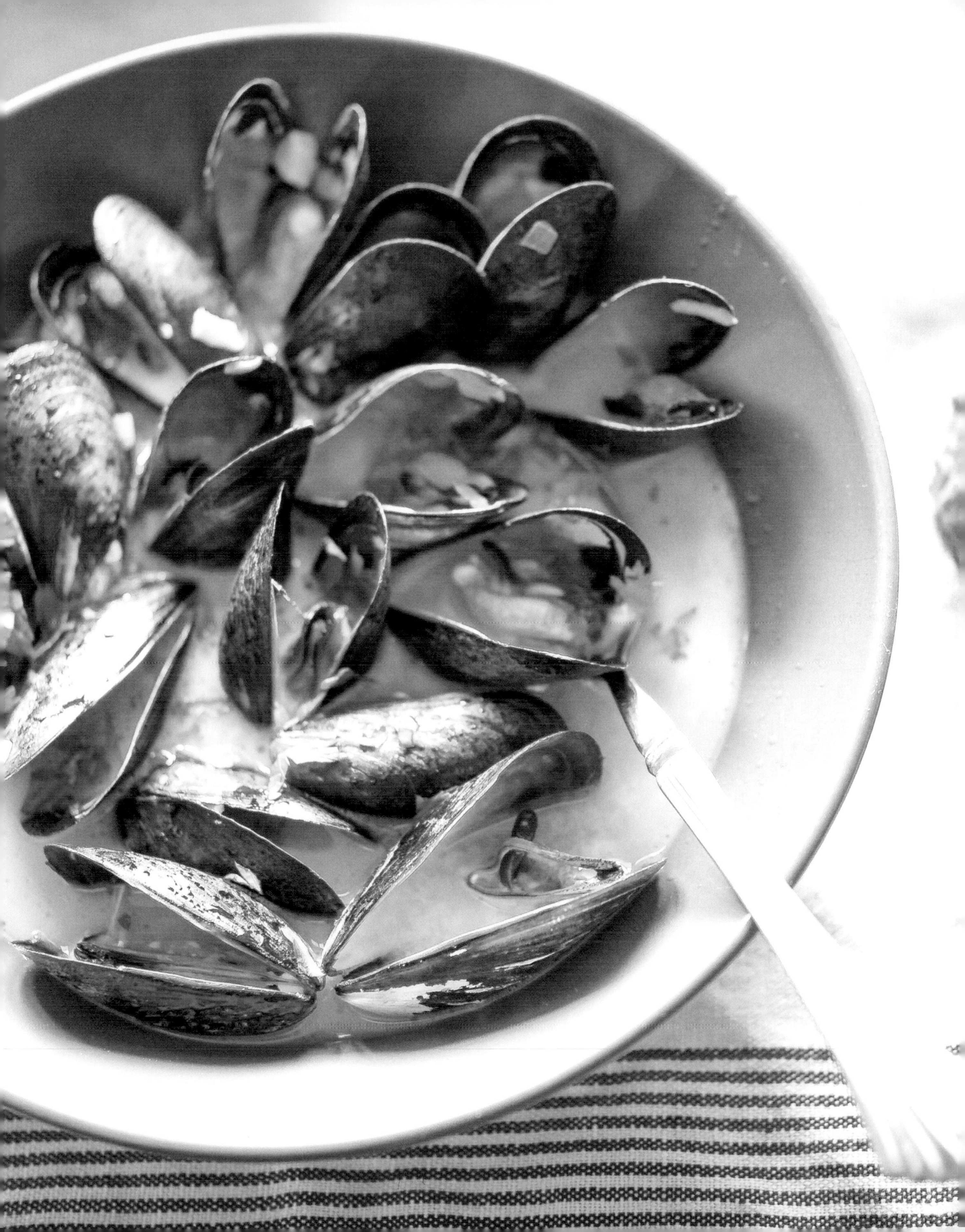

Dijon & Herb
ALMOND-CRUSTED SNAPPER

Yield: 4 servings   *Prep time:* 10 minutes   *Cook time:* 25 minutes

My Dijon herb coating transforms boring whitefish, making this dish so tasty that the whole family will love it. Almond flour makes a great substitute for the breadcrumbs commonly used to coat foods.

⅔ cup almond flour

Leaves from 2 sprigs of fresh flat-leaf parsley, chopped

½ teaspoon fine sea salt

¼ cup Dijon mustard

2 cloves garlic, chopped

1 tablespoon raw honey

2 (8-ounce) snapper fillets, halved

1. Preheat the oven to 400°F. Line a rimmed baking sheet with parchment paper.

2. In a medium-sized bowl, mix together the almond flour, parsley, and salt.

3. In a separate small bowl, whisk together the mustard, garlic, and honey.

4. Spread the mustard mixture all over the fish fillets, then dip each fillet in the flour mixture and place on the prepared baking sheet.

5. Bake for 25 minutes, or until the fish is flaky and opaque and the coating is lightly toasted.

Spicy Vietnamese
RAINBOW TROUT

Yield: 4 servings   *Prep time:* 5 minutes   *Cook time:* 10 minutes

Rainbow trout gets a sweet and spicy makeover in this dish. Coconut palm sugar and water create a very light syrup that is freshened up with lemon juice and ginger. Fish sauce, a staple in Vietnamese cooking, contributes an umami flavor.

3 tablespoons water

1 tablespoon coconut palm sugar or cane sugar

2 teaspoons fresh grated ginger

1½ teaspoons fresh lemon juice

1½ teaspoons fish sauce

½ teaspoon red pepper flakes

2 skin-on rainbow trout fillets (about 1½ pounds)

¼ teaspoon fine sea salt

1. In a 12-inch skillet, place the water, coconut palm sugar, ginger, lemon juice, fish sauce, and red pepper flakes. Turn the heat to medium and stir.

2. Sprinkle the trout fillets with the salt. Place the fish skin side down in the pan and cover with a lid. Simmer for 10 minutes, or until the fish flakes and is opaque.

3. Place the fish on a platter and drizzle with the pan sauce to serve.

Ginger Beef
STIR-FRY

Yield: 4 servings   *Prep time:* 10 minutes, plus at least 30 minutes to marinate
Cook time: 5 minutes, plus 15 minutes for the cauliflower rice

This quick dish is loaded with nutritious vegetables and bone broth. If you don't have homemade beef bone broth on hand, you can always use store-bought beef broth instead. Any cut of steak will work, but I prefer sirloin.

FOR THE MARINADE:

¼ cup coconut aminos

2 tablespoons coconut palm sugar

2 tablespoons finely chopped fresh ginger

2 tablespoons unseasoned rice vinegar

2 pounds top sirloin steak, sliced thinly against the grain

FOR THE SAUCE:

2 cups Beef Bone Broth (page 77)

¼ cup plus 2 tablespoons arrowroot starch

¼ cup plus 2 tablespoons coconut aminos

3 tablespoons coconut palm sugar

2 cloves garlic, minced

1 tablespoon plus 1 teaspoon finely chopped fresh ginger

4 tablespoons extra-virgin olive oil, divided

2 cups chopped broccoli

1 onion, cut into 1-inch pieces

1 red bell pepper, cut into 1-inch pieces

1 recipe Cauliflower Rice (page 272), for serving

1. In a resealable bag, combine the ingredients for the marinade. Add the steak and shake to coat. Seal the bag and refrigerate for at least 30 minutes or up to 24 hours.

2. Mix together the sauce ingredients in a bowl and set aside.

3. After the steak is done marinating, heat 2 tablespoons of the olive oil in a large skillet or wok over medium-high heat. Place the steak in the hot skillet and fry for 2 to 3 minutes, until cooked through, stirring often. Remove the steak from the skillet and set aside.

4. Add the remaining 2 tablespoons of olive oil and the broccoli, onion, and bell pepper to the skillet and sauté for 2 minutes.

5. Return the steak to the skillet and reduce the heat to medium-low. Whisk the sauce and pour it over the beef. Give everything a quick stir and cook for 1 minute. The sauce will begin to thicken immediately.

6. Serve over cauliflower rice.

Smoky Chipotle Aioli Burgers with
CRUNCHY MANGO SLAW

Yield: 4 servings   *Prep time:* 10 minutes   *Cook time:* 16 minutes

Here are the two secrets to making great burgers: First, don't overmix the meat; instead, mix it until it is just combined. Second, do not take a spatula and push down on the meat to make the burgers cook faster; this only dries out the meat, and no one wants a dry burger. Since I don't consume cheese, I like to top my burgers with aioli or guacamole instead.

FOR THE SLAW:

½ mango, peeled and thinly sliced

1 cup finely shredded purple cabbage

FOR THE BURGERS:

4 tablespoons extra-virgin olive oil, divided

½ medium onion, chopped

2 pounds lean ground beef

1 teaspoon fine sea salt

½ teaspoon ground black pepper

4 Sandwich Buns (page 132) or large lettuce leaves, for wrapping

½ cup Smoky Chipotle Aioli (page 66)

ADDITIONAL TOPPINGS (OPTIONAL):

Lettuce leaves (if using buns)

Sliced tomato

Sliced red onion

Cooked bacon slices

1. Make the slaw: Place the mango and cabbage in a small bowl and toss together. Set aside at room temperature while you make the burgers. During this time the juice from the mango will soften the cabbage.

2. Heat 2 tablespoons of the olive oil in a 12-inch cast-iron skillet over medium-high heat. Place the onion in the hot pan and sauté until translucent, about 10 minutes.

3. Pour the cooked onion into a medium-sized bowl. Add the beef, salt, and pepper and mix until just combined.

4. Form into four ½-inch-thick burgers. Use your thumb to press an indentation into the middle of each burger.

5. Heat the remaining 2 tablespoons of olive oil in the same skillet over medium heat. Place the burgers in the hot skillet. Cook for 5 minutes per side for medium-rare or 6 to 7 minutes per side for fully cooked burgers.

6. Serve in homemade buns or wrapped in large lettuce leaves, topped with the slaw and aioli and any additional toppings of your choice.

Thyme Dijon Mustard
PRIME RIB

Yield: 6 to 8 servings   *Prep time:* 10 minutes   *Cook time:* 2 hours 10 minutes

I prefer to cook large pieces of meat using the reverse-sear technique. Normally you sear the meat first, either in a large skillet or in a hot oven, to form a crust, then you turn the heat down and allow the roast to cook slowly. The reverse-sear technique switches it around: you sear the meat at the end. This option is great if you are hosting a party because you can cook the meat ahead of time and then pop it back in the oven for the sear and it will taste perfect.

FOR THE MUSTARD-THYME RUB:

¼ cup (½ stick) unsalted butter or ghee (page 56)

¼ cup Dijon mustard

¼ cup peeled and grated fresh horseradish root (about 2 ounces) (see Notes)

¼ cup fresh thyme leaves

5 cloves garlic, peeled and chopped

1 teaspoon fine sea salt

½ teaspoon ground black pepper

1 (5- to 6-pound) prime rib roast

FOR THE PAN SAUCE:

Pan drippings (from roast, above; see Notes)

2 cups Beef Bone Broth (page 77)

¼ cup unsalted butter, chilled, diced (omit for dairy-free; see Notes)

1. Preheat the oven to 300°F.

2. Place all the ingredients for the rub in a food processor and puree to form a paste. Rub the paste all over the roast.

3. Place the roast in a roasting pan. Roast until the internal temperature reaches 110°F for rare, about 1½ hours, or 115°F for medium-rare, 10 minutes longer.

4. Increase the heat to 475°F and roast for 10 minutes, or until the internal temperature reaches 125°F for rare or 130°F for medium-rare.

5. Remove from the oven and move the roast onto a cutting board; set the roasting pan aside (you will be using it momentarily.) Allow the meat to rest for 20 minutes.

6. Begin making the pan sauce 15 minutes prior to serving the meat. Place the roasting pan with the pan drippings on the stove, add the bone broth, and turn the heat to medium. Cook the sauce for 10 minutes, stirring often. Reduce the heat to the lowest setting to keep the sauce warm (do not allow it to simmer) and gradually add the chilled butter, whisking constantly; the sauce will thicken slightly and take on a beautiful sheen. Immediately pour the sauce into a gravy boat and serve with the meat.

Notes: *If your prime rib roast is 100 percent grass-fed, it's possible that you will not have much in the way of pan drippings; simply proceed with the recipe as written but add ¼ cup more broth.*

To make the pan sauce dairy-free, omit the butter and make a slurry with 2 teaspoons of arrowroot starch and 2 teaspoons of water. Whisk the slurry into the sauce in Step 6.

When shopping for horseradish, look for a root that is clean and firm. To grate fresh horseradish, hold the peeled and trimmed horseradish root and rub it against a fine grating surface using a downward crisscross motion. Be aware that ground-up fresh horseradish is very potent and can really hurt your eyes if you get too close to the fumes.

Meatloaf with
MAPLE BALSAMIC GLAZE

Yield: 4 servings   Prep time: 15 minutes   Cook time: 1 hour 20 minutes

I am a huge fan of meatloaf. Not only is it a budget-friendly way to use grass-fed beef, it's also an easy-to-make, tasty dish that lets you have dinner ready in a relatively short time. The glaze is a simplified version of my favorite homemade barbecue sauce; it is sweet with a hint of tanginess from the balsamic vinegar.

FOR THE GLAZE:

¼ cup tomato paste

1 tablespoon balsamic vinegar

1 tablespoon maple syrup

FOR THE MEATLOAF:

2 tablespoons ghee (page 56)

1 medium onion, finely chopped

1 stalk celery, finely chopped

2 cups finely chopped white mushrooms (about 8 mushrooms)

1 pound lean ground beef

1 pound ground pork

2 large eggs

2 teaspoons dried parsley

1½ teaspoons garlic powder

1 teaspoon fine sea salt

½ teaspoon ground black pepper

1. Preheat the oven to 350°F.

2. In a small bowl, combine the glaze ingredients.

3. Heat the ghee in a 12-inch skillet over medium heat. Add the onion, celery, and mushrooms and cook until the onion is translucent, about 10 minutes, stirring often.

4. In a large bowl, mix together half of the glaze, the cooked vegetables, and the remaining meatloaf ingredients. Place the meat mixture in an 8-by-4-inch loaf pan and form it into a log.

5. Bake the meatloaf for 55 minutes, then remove from the oven. Drain the fat into a bowl and discard. Use a pastry brush to brush the rest of the glaze on the meatloaf, making sure to cover the top evenly.

6. Bake for another 15 minutes, or until the juices from the meat run clear.

Swedish
MEATBALLS

Yield: 4 servings *Prep time:* 10 minutes *Cook time:* 1 hour

I had my first Swedish meatball at IKEA, and it became a tradition to eat Swedish meatballs every time I visited that store. I loved the unique taste of those little meatballs accompanied by a delicious gravy. For this Paleo version, I created a dairy-free gravy with coconut milk, and trust me, you can't tell that it's made with coconut milk.

FOR THE MEATBALLS:

2 tablespoons ghee (page 56)

2 cups finely chopped white mushrooms (about 8 mushrooms)

1 cup finely chopped onions

2 pounds ground pork

2 large eggs

¼ teaspoon ground allspice

¼ teaspoon ground nutmeg

1 teaspoon fine sea salt

½ teaspoon ground black pepper

FOR THE GRAVY:

2 cups Beef Bone Broth (page 77)

1 cup full-fat coconut milk

½ teaspoon fine sea salt

¼ teaspoon ground black pepper

1 tablespoon arrowroot starch, plus 1 tablespoon more if desired

1 tablespoon water, plus 1 tablespoon more if desired

¼ cup chopped fresh flat-leaf parsley, for garnish

1. In a large skillet, melt the ghee over medium heat. Add the mushrooms and onions and sauté until the onions are translucent and the mushrooms have softened, about 10 minutes.

2. Transfer the cooked onions and mushrooms to a medium-sized bowl. Let cool slightly, then add the pork, eggs, allspice, nutmeg, salt, and pepper and mix until thoroughly combined.

3. Roll the meat into about twenty-eight 1½-inch balls.

4. Place half the meatballs in the same skillet you used to cook the onions and mushrooms. Cook over medium heat for 20 minutes, or until the meat is no longer pink in the center, turning once. Remove the cooked meatballs from the skillet.

5. Repeat with the second batch of raw meatballs.

6. Make the gravy: Place all the gravy ingredients except the arrowroot starch and water in the same skillet and bring to a boil. Continue boiling, whisking occasionally, for 5 minutes.

7. In a small bowl, make a slurry by whisking together the arrowroot starch and water. Pour the slurry into the gravy while whisking quickly. If you desire a thicker gravy, repeat the process with an additional tablespoon of arrowroot starch mixed with a tablespoon of water. Strain the gravy before serving.

8. Serve the gravy over the meatballs. Garnish with parsley.

Beef Tongue
TACOS

Yield: 12 tacos (4 servings)   Prep time: 5 minutes   Cook time: 8 hours

This is a very easy recipe for incorporating organ meat into your diet. Don't be intimidated by beef tongue and its unique look. You don't eat the skin; you peel it off, and inside is the most tender meat. You can find beef tongue at your local butcher shop, or ask your local cattle farmer (the one who pastures his or her own cattle!).

1 beef tongue

Fine sea salt and ground black pepper

2 recipes Grain-Free Tortillas (page 130)

2 avocados, thinly sliced

1 cup Salsa (page 68)

¼ cup fresh cilantro leaves, chopped

1 lime, quartered

1. Place the beef tongue in a 6-quart slow cooker. Fill with water and turn the heat to low. Cook for at least 8 hours.

2. Remove the beef tongue and place it on a cutting board. Use a knife to cut a slit in the skin, then peel off the skin and discard it.

3. Use two forks to shred the beef and place it in a medium-sized mixing bowl. Sprinkle the shredded beef with salt and pepper.

4. Serve the shredded beef in the tortillas and top with the avocados, salsa, cilantro, and a squeeze of lime juice.

Chicken Fingers with
DIPPING SAUCE

Yield: 4 servings   *Prep time:* 10 minutes   *Cook time:* 30 minutes

My favorite way to eat chicken breast is to turn it into chicken fingers. I love the crunchy coating, and I love dipping them into a yummy, creamy sauce like Smoky Chipotle Aioli (page 66). This dish pairs well with Oven-Baked Sweet Potato Fries (page 274) and coleslaw.

---

4 (6-ounce) boneless, skinless chicken breasts

2 large eggs

3 cups almond flour

1 tablespoon fine sea salt

1 tablespoon paprika

1½ teaspoons garlic powder

1½ teaspoons onion powder

1½ teaspoons dried oregano

1½ teaspoons dried rubbed sage

½ teaspoon ground black pepper

1 recipe Smoky Chipotle Aioli (page 66), for serving

1. Preheat the oven to 400°F. Line a rimmed baking sheet with parchment paper.

2. Cut each chicken breast lengthwise into 4 or 5 long strips.

3. In a medium-sized bowl, whisk the eggs.

4. In another medium-sized bowl, mix together the almond flour, salt, and seasonings until combined.

5. Place the chicken strips in the bowl with the eggs and toss until evenly coated. Then dip each strip in the seasoned almond flour. Place the coated chicken fingers on the prepared baking sheet.

6. Bake for 30 minutes, or until the juices run clear. Serve with Smoky Chipotle Aioli for dipping.

Cilantro Maple Sriracha
CHICKEN WINGS

Yield: 4 servings   Prep time: 10 minutes   Cook time: 35 minutes

I love scorching-hot sauces on my chicken wings—the kind where you know it's torture to take another bite, but you do it anyway because you love the taste. For this recipe, I used my favorite hot sauce, Sriracha, and sweetened it a little with maple syrup. The cilantro will help cool down your mouth.

FOR THE SPICE BLEND:

1 teaspoon garlic powder

1 teaspoon paprika

1 teaspoon fine sea salt

½ teaspoon cayenne pepper

½ teaspoon ginger powder

½ teaspoon ground black pepper

28 chicken wing pieces (14 drumettes, 14 wing tips)

¼ cup extra-virgin olive oil

¼ cup Sriracha sauce, homemade (page 96) or store-bought

¼ cup maple syrup

¼ cup chopped fresh cilantro, for garnish

1. Preheat the oven to 400°F. Line a rimmed baking sheet with parchment paper.

2. In a small bowl, combine the garlic powder, paprika, salt, cayenne, ginger powder, and black pepper.

3. Place the chicken wing pieces in a large bowl. Pour the olive oil over the wings, then sprinkle them with the spice blend. Toss to evenly coat.

4. Place the wings on the lined baking sheet and bake for 35 minutes, or until they are no longer pink inside and the juices run clear, flipping once.

5. Whisk together the Sriracha sauce and maple syrup in a small bowl. Place the cooked wings in a separate bowl. Pour the sauce over the wings and toss to evenly coat.

6. Sprinkle the wings with the cilantro and serve.

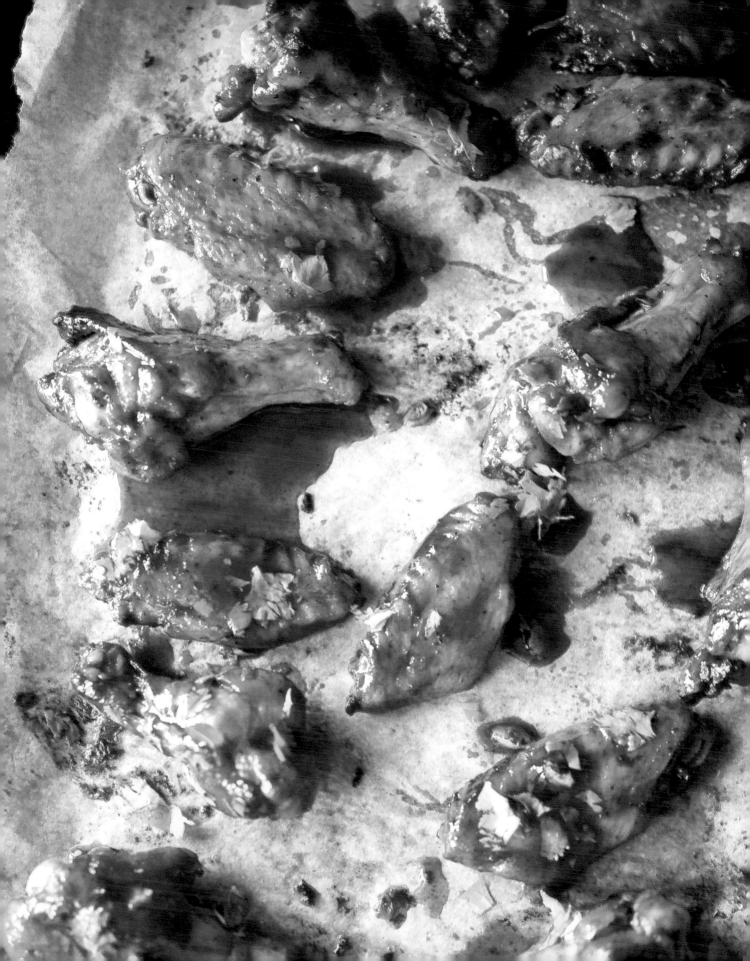

Lemon Rosemary
ROAST CHICKEN

Yield: 4 servings   *Prep time:* 10 minutes   *Cook time:* 1½ hours

This simple roast chicken recipe gives you crispy skin and moist meat. Stuffing the chicken with rosemary, lemon, onion, and garlic infuses it with flavor.

1 (4- to 5-pound) whole chicken

Fine sea salt and ground black pepper

2 tablespoons unsalted butter, melted, or preferred fat

1 lemon, cut into wedges

½ medium onion, cut into wedges

6 cloves garlic, peeled

5 sprigs fresh rosemary

1. Preheat the oven to 425°F.

2. Pat the chicken skin dry with a paper towel. Season the inside with salt and pepper. Pour the melted butter over the chicken and rub it all over. Sprinkle salt and pepper all over the chicken. Stuff the cavity with the lemon, onion, garlic, and rosemary. Tie the legs together.

3. Place the chicken in a roasting pan, breast side up, and roast for 1½ hours, basting often. The chicken is done when a thermometer inserted into the thickest part of the thigh reads 165°F.

4. Let the chicken rest for 10 minutes before carving. Remove the aromatics from the cavity and discard.

Dairy-Free
BUTTER CHICKEN

Yield: 4 servings *Prep time:* 5 minutes *Cook time:* 35 minutes, plus 15 minutes for the cauliflower rice

One day at work, Rob, a coworker, was describing how he makes homemade butter chicken. He talked about how he toasts the spices in a skillet, filling the kitchen with the most delicious aroma. I was sold. I went home and immediately worked on a dairy-free version. Here's my tested-till-perfect dairy-free butter chicken.

2 tablespoons extra-virgin olive oil

2 (6-ounce) boneless, skinless chicken breasts, cut into 1-inch pieces

½ cup chopped onions

4 cloves garlic, finely chopped

1 tablespoon ginger powder

2 teaspoons curry powder

1 teaspoon fine sea salt

½ teaspoon ground cinnamon

½ teaspoon garam masala

¼ teaspoon chili powder

¼ teaspoon ground black pepper

2 cups Chicken Bone Broth (page 77)

1 cup coconut cream (see page 33)

¼ cup tomato paste

1 recipe Cauliflower Rice (page 272), for serving

Fresh flat-leaf parsley, for garnish

1. Heat the olive oil in a 12-inch skillet over medium heat. Place the chicken in the hot pan and cook, stirring occasionally, until no longer pink, about 6 minutes.

2. Remove the chicken from the pan. Add the onions and garlic and cook until translucent, about 10 minutes. Add the ginger, curry powder, salt, cinnamon, garam masala, chili powder, and pepper and cook for 2 minutes.

3. Add the bone broth, coconut cream, tomato paste, and cooked chicken and cook for at least 15 minutes, stirring occasionally. The butter chicken is done when the sauce is thick. Serve immediately over cauliflower rice, garnished with parsley.

Honey Mustard Garlic
CHICKEN THIGHS

Yield: 4 servings *Prep time:* 10 minutes *Cook time:* 45 minutes

If you like honey mustard sauce, you'll love this chicken thigh dish. I like to serve it during the week along with pureed cauliflower and a salad for an easy, no-fuss meal.

4 bone-in, skin-on chicken thighs

Fine sea salt and ground black pepper

⅔ cup Dijon mustard

⅓ cup raw honey

4 cloves garlic, chopped

1. Preheat the oven to 375°F.

2. Place the chicken thighs in a baking dish and season with salt and pepper.

3. In a small bowl, whisk together the mustard, honey, and garlic. Pour the sauce over the chicken thighs.

4. Bake for 45 minutes, or until the meat is no longer pink and the juices run clear, basting occasionally.

Hungarian Cabbage ROLLS

Yield: 4 servings   *Prep time:* 20 minutes   *Cook time:* 4½ hours

My family's recipe for Hungarian cabbage rolls is a treasured secret that's requested year after year at family gatherings. My grandmother taught my mother how to make the cabbage rolls, and then my mother, who added barbecue spice to the rolls for more flavor, passed the recipe to me when I was a teenager. For the longest time, I was only allowed to mix the meat mixture. Eventually I graduated to the sacred job of filling the cabbage leaves with the meat mixture and perfectly tucking in each cabbage leaf. Now I pass my family's recipe on to you, with only one small change: traditionally cabbage rolls are made with rice, but for Paleo purposes I've eliminated that here.

2 small heads cabbage

2 tablespoons extra-virgin olive oil

½ medium onion, minced

½ pound lean ground beef

½ pound ground pork

½ teaspoon BBQ Spice Mix (page 170; optional)

½ teaspoon garlic powder

¼ teaspoon paprika

½ teaspoon fine sea salt

¼ teaspoon ground black pepper

1 (46-ounce) can tomato juice, divided

1 (24-ounce) jar pasta sauce

1. Using a knife, make four deep cuts around the core of each head of cabbage, but leave the core intact (see figures 1 and 2).

2. Place the cabbage in a 12-quart pot filled with water. The water needs to cover the cabbage. Boil until the cabbage leaves are soft and bendable, about 20 minutes.

3. While the cabbage is boiling, prepare the filling: Heat the olive oil in an 8-inch skillet over medium heat. Place the onion in the hot pan and sauté until translucent, about 10 minutes. Remove from the heat and let cool slightly.

4. In a large mixing bowl, mix the sautéed onion with the ground beef, ground pork, barbecue spice (if using), garlic powder, paprika, salt, and pepper.

5. Mix ¼ cup of the tomato juice into the meat. This will ensure that the meat stays moist.

6. Use a fork to gently separate the leaves from the core of the cabbage while it's still in the pot. Remove the leaves from the pot, placing the outermost leaves on one tray and the inner leaves on another tray (see figure 3).

7. Line the bottom of a large slow cooker with the outer cabbage leaves. This will help prevent the cabbage rolls from burning (see figure 4).

8. Prep the cabbage leaves: Use only medium-sized and small cabbage leaves to make the rolls. Take a cabbage leaf and slice off the stiff stem (see figure 5). Trim any uneven edges; you want the leaf fairly even on all sides.

(cont. on page 244)

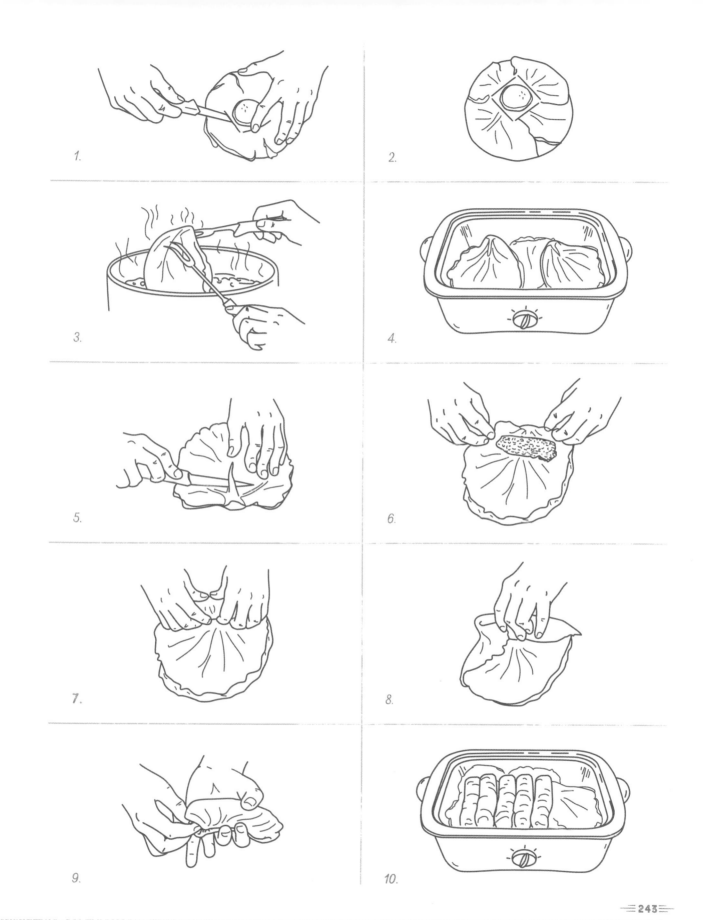

1.

2.

3.

4.

5.

6.

7.

8.

9.

10.

9. Fill and roll the leaves: Take a small handful of the meat mixture, form it into a cigar shape, and place it across the top of a cabbage leaf, near the stem (see figure 6). Fold the stem end over the filling and begin to roll the leaf up (see figure 7) until the filling is snug and secured, then fold in one side of the leaf (see figure 8) and finishing rolling up the leaf. Use your finger to tuck the open side of the leaf inside to seal the roll (see figure 9). If there is an excess amount of uneven cabbage leaf at the end of the open side, trim it off to get a clean edge. You need about 1½ inches of extra cabbage leaf at the end to properly seal the roll.

10. Place the cabbage roll seam side down in the slow cooker. Repeat with the remaining cabbage leaves and meat mixture, arranging the rolls in neat rows (see figure 10).

11. Mix together the remaining tomato juice and the pasta sauce.

12. Pour the sauce over the cabbage rolls in the slow cooker, making sure to cover all the rolls. If there isn't enough sauce, add water until all the cabbage rolls are covered.

13. Turn the slow cooker to high until the sauce boils. Then turn the heat to low and continue cooking for about 4 hours, or until the meat inside the cabbage rolls is cooked.

Smoky Pineapple
PULLED PORK

Yield: 6 servings   *Prep time:* 5 minutes   *Cook time:* 6½ hours

I love a simple meal, and this one is as simple as it gets. The slow cooker does all the work. The barbecue sauce I paired with the pork is tropical with a touch of smokiness. You can serve pulled pork in many ways: on Sandwich Buns (page 132), in lettuce wraps, or in Grain-Free Tortillas (page 130) for pulled pork tacos.

1 (2- to 3-pound) bone-in pork shoulder

Fine sea salt and ground black pepper

1 recipe Smoky Pineapple BBQ Sauce (page 74)

1 recipe Sandwich Buns (page 132), for serving (optional; omit for egg- and nut-free)

6 slices grilled fresh pineapple, for serving (optional; see Note)

1. Season the pork with salt and pepper. Place it in a 6-quart slow cooker, cover with water, and turn the heat to low. Cook for at least 6 hours, until the meat can easily be shredded with a fork.

2. Remove the pork from the slow cooker, discard the water, and place the pork in a large bowl. Use two forks to shred the meat.

3. Toss the shredded pork with the Smoky Pineapple BBQ Sauce. Place the sauced meat back in the slow cooker and heat on low for at least 30 minutes to allow the flavors to saturate the meat.

4. Ladle the pulled pork onto buns and top with grilled pineapple slices, if desired.

Note: For grilled pineapple slices, first cut a freshly cored pineapple into six ¼-inch-thick slices. Brush a cast-iron grill pan or a barbecue grill with olive oil. Turn the heat to medium. Once the grill is hot, place the pineapple slices on it and cook for 2 to 3 minutes, until you can see grill marks. Flip and cook for another 2 to 3 minutes.

Apple Butter
BBQ RIBS

Yield: 4 servings   *Prep time:* 5 minutes   *Cook time:* 2 hours 5 minutes

These ribs are falling-off-the-bone delicious! And since they're cooked in the oven, you can make them any time of the year. Sealing the ribs in a package prevents the meat from drying out and gives you tender, juicy ribs. Use my smoky Apple Butter BBQ Sauce (page 72) to make them irresistible.

2 racks baby back pork ribs or pork back ribs

Fine sea salt and ground black pepper

1 recipe Apple Butter BBQ Sauce (page 72)

1. Place an oven rack in the middle position. Preheat the oven to 325°F.

2. Prepare the ribs by scoring the membrane on the back: Take a sharp knife and lightly cut into the membrane at a 90-degree angle, spacing the cuts about 1 inch apart. Season the ribs with salt and pepper.

3. Wrap the ribs in aluminum foil, bone side down, creating a tightly sealed package. Place the package on a rimmed baking sheet and bake for 2 hours, or until the meat is falling off the bones.

4. Remove the ribs from the foil and place them back on the rimmed baking sheet. Spread the Apple Butter BBQ Sauce on the ribs.

5. Return the ribs to the oven and turn the broiler to high heat. Broil until the top is lightly charred and the sauce is bubbling, about 5 minutes. Brush with more sauce, if desired.

6. Cut the ribs into sections and serve immediately.

Spinach, Raisin & Pine Nut-Stuffed
PORK LOIN

Yield: 4 servings *Prep time:* 20 minutes *Cook time:* 1½ hours

This pork loin recipe is elevated by a stuffing that is both savory and sweet. The pan sauce that accompanies it is the most delicious sauce you will ever eat, and the butter makes it creamy and rich.

1 (2-pound) boneless pork loin

2 tablespoons extra-virgin olive oil

2 cups baby spinach, stems removed

½ cup chopped onions

½ cup chopped shiitake mushrooms (about 1 ounce)

¼ cup pine nuts

¼ cup raisins

2 cloves garlic, chopped

1 tablespoon chopped fresh sage

Fine sea salt and ground black pepper

8 slices bacon

FOR THE PAN SAUCE:

Pan drippings (from the pork loin, above)

2 cups Chicken Bone Broth (page 77)

1 tablespoon raw apple cider vinegar

1 teaspoon Dijon mustard

2 teaspoons arrowroot starch

2 teaspoons water

¼ cup (½ stick) unsalted butter, chilled, diced (omit for dairy-free; see Note opposite page)

1. Preheat the oven to 300°F.

2. Butterfly the pork loin: Place the pork fat side down on the right side of a large cutting board (or the left side if you are left-handed). With your knife positioned parallel to the cutting board and beginning along one long side, start by cutting about ½ inch deep into the meat. Continue gently slicing along that same line while "unrolling" the meat, until you create a flap of meat that lies flat on the cutting board. You will end up with a large, flat piece of meat onto which you can place the stuffing and then roll it back up. Be careful not to cut all the way through at the end or you will end up with two flat pieces of pork loin, not one butterflied piece. (See figures 1, 2, and 3.)

3. Heat the olive oil in a 12-inch skillet over medium heat. Sauté the spinach, onions, mushrooms, pine nuts, raisins, garlic, and sage for 5 minutes, stirring often, and season with salt and pepper.

4. Spread the spinach mixture on top of the butterflied pork, making sure to keep the stuffing about 1 inch away from the sides. Tightly roll it back together.

5. Place the bacon strips on the fat side of the pork loin, season with salt and pepper, and use butcher's twine to hold the roast together.

6. Place the roast in a roasting pan and roast until the internal temperature reaches 145°F, about 1 hour.

7. Increase the heat to 475°F and roast for 10 minutes, or until the internal temperature reaches 155°F.

8. Remove the roast from the oven and allow it to rest for 20 minutes on a cutting board. Leave the pan drippings in the pan.

9. Make the pan sauce: About 15 minutes prior to serving the meat, place the roasting pan with the pan drippings on the stovetop over medium heat. Add the bone broth, vinegar, and mustard and cook for 10 minutes, stirring often. While the sauce is cooking, make a slurry by whisking together the arrowroot starch and water in a small bowl.

10. After 10 minutes, reduce the heat to the lowest setting to keep the sauce warm (do not allow it to simmer) and gradually add the chilled butter, whisking constantly; the sauce will thicken slightly and take on a beautiful sheen.

11. Whisk in the slurry. The sauce will thicken immediately. Pour the sauce into a gravy boat and serve with the meat.

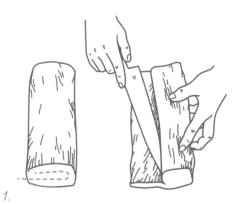

1.

2.

3.

Note: To make the pan sauce dairy-free, omit the butter and use more arrowroot starch, adding the starch in 1-teaspoon increments until the sauce reaches your desired thickness.

Thyme Mushroom
PORK CHOPS

Yield: 4 servings   *Prep time:* 10 minutes   *Cook time:* 24 minutes

This elegant pork chop recipe looks complicated, but it's actually very easy to make.

2 tablespoons extra-virgin olive oil

4 bone-in pork chops (about ½ inch thick)

Fine sea salt and ground black pepper

12 white mushrooms, sliced (about 3 cups), divided

4 sprigs fresh thyme, divided

½ medium onion, chopped, divided

2 cloves garlic, chopped, divided

2 tablespoons unsalted butter, divided

1. Heat the olive oil in a 12-inch skillet over medium heat.

2. Season the pork chops with salt and pepper. Cover two chops. Place the other two in the hot skillet and cook for 5 to 6 minutes, then flip the meat and add half of the mushrooms, thyme, onion, and garlic.

3. Place 1 tablespoon of the butter in the pan. Once melted, spoon the butter over the meat. Cook for an additional 5 to 6 minutes, until the flesh is no longer pink, stirring the vegetables occasionally.

4. Remove the meat and vegetables from pan and set aside. Repeat Steps 2 and 3 with the remaining two pork chops and vegetables.

5. Discard the thyme sprigs. Serve the meat with the mushrooms spooned over it.

Creamy Tomato Mushroom
CHICKEN PASTA

Yield: 4 servings   *Prep time:* 15 minutes   *Cook time:* 20 minutes

You can use vegetables and starches to make noodles for your favorite pasta dishes. Vegetable-based noodles are an easy way to eat more vegetables. To make the noodles, use a vegetable peeler or a tool called a spiral slicer (see page 38).

FOR THE SAUCE:

1 cup tomato sauce

1 cup coconut cream (see page 33)

4 medium zucchinis, peeled

Fine sea salt and ground black pepper

4 slices bacon, chopped

½ medium onion, chopped

8 white mushrooms, sliced (about 2 cups)

4 cloves garlic, chopped

2 (6-ounce) boneless, skinless chicken breasts, cut into 1-inch pieces

2 tablespoons chopped fresh flat-leaf parsley, for garnish (optional)

1. Make the sauce: In a small bowl, mix together the tomato sauce and coconut cream and set aside. The sauce will be a light red color.

2. Use a spiral slicer to create zucchini noodles, following the instructions for the machine. If you don't have a spiral slicer, use a vegetable peeler to create long, flat strands of zucchini. Place the noodles in a large bowl, sprinkle liberally with salt, and toss. Set the noodles aside while you prepare the rest of the ingredients. The salt will draw out excess water from the noodles.

3. Place the bacon, onion, mushrooms, and garlic in a large skillet over medium heat. Sauté for 10 minutes, or until the bacon is crispy, stirring often. Using a slotted spoon, remove the bacon and vegetables from the pan and set aside, leaving the bacon fat in the pan.

4. Add the chicken to the hot pan, season with a generous pinch of salt and pepper, and sauté for 5 minutes, or until the chicken is no longer pink inside, stirring occasionally.

5. Rinse the salt off the zucchini noodles, drain, and gently pat dry with paper towels.

6. Return the bacon and vegetables to the skillet and add the zucchini noodles. Add the sauce and simmer for 5 minutes, or until the noodles are heated through.

7. Add salt and pepper to taste. Garnish with chopped fresh parsley, if desired, and serve immediately.

Mango Prosciutto
GRAIN-FREE PIZZA

Yield: 4 servings *Prep time:* 10 minutes *Cook time:* 35 minutes

This sweet, spicy, and salty pizza is my fancy version of Hawaiian pizza.

FOR THE CRUST:

2 large eggs

2 cups tapioca starch, plus more as needed

1 cup full-fat coconut milk

¾ cup sifted coconut flour

½ cup extra-virgin olive oil

1 tablespoon instant yeast (see Note)

½ teaspoon cream of tartar

¼ teaspoon baking soda

¼ teaspoon fine sea salt

TOPPINGS:

¼ cup pizza sauce

½ mango, peeled and thinly sliced

¼ cup pickled or fermented jalapeño peppers, homemade (page 94) or store-bought

¼ red onion, thinly sliced

4 slices prosciutto, torn into small pieces

Special equipment:

Pizza stone

1. Preheat the oven to 350°F. Line a pizza stone with parchment paper.

2. In a medium-sized bowl, mix together all the crust ingredients. Keep mixing until a dough forms. The dough will resemble a batter.

3. Place the dough on the pizza stone and use your hands or a spatula to spread it out, sprinkling more tapioca starch on the dough if needed. Create an 11-inch circle, leaving the edges slightly higher.

4. Bake for 20 minutes, then remove the crust from the oven. Increase the oven temperature to 450°F.

5. Spread the pizza sauce all over the crust. Top with the remaining pizza toppings and bake for an additional 15 minutes.

6. Slice the pizza and serve immediately.

Note: Remember that instant yeast and active dry yeast aren't exactly the same. Instant yeast has a fine texture and can be added directly to dry ingredients. Active dry yeast has larger granules and needs to be dissolved before using. And keep in mind that neither is the same as nutritional yeast, which is used in other recipes to give a dish a cheesy flavor—it won't make anything rise.

Don't worry if the crust on the finished pizza looks a little undercooked. When the sauce and toppings touch the high-starch, nut- and grain-free dough, the added liquid can make the top part of the pizza crust look gel-like.

Grain-Free
LASAGNA

Yield: 8 servings *Prep time:* 30 minutes, plus 30 minutes to chill the cheese
Cook time: 1 hour 20 minutes

This grain-free lasagna uses ripe plantains as a base for the noodles. (Don't worry, you won't be able to taste the plantains in the cooked lasagna.) Make sure you use ripe plantains, which have skins that are yellow with black spots and peel off easily. Unripe plantains are green, just like unripe bananas. If the plantains are all black, they are too ripe for this recipe. Note that, instead of boiling individual strips of lasagna dough before assembly, this lasagna is created with three large single sheets of dough. I have provided a filling that I like to use, but you can substitute your favorite filling if you prefer.

FOR THE DAIRY-FREE CHEESE:

2 cups raw cashews

1¼ cups hot water

¾ cup arrowroot starch

2 tablespoons fresh lemon juice

2 tablespoons grass-fed unflavored gelatin

½ teaspoon fine sea salt

FOR THE DOUGH:

1½ pounds ripe plantains (about 2 large) (see headnote)

2¼ cups arrowroot starch, plus more if needed

1 cup almond flour

¼ teaspoon fine sea salt

FOR THE FILLING:

2 pounds lean ground beef

2 teaspoons fine sea salt

1 teaspoon ground black pepper

2 medium onions, chopped

2 cups chopped white mushrooms (about 8 mushrooms)

2 cloves garlic, chopped

2 (24-ounce) jars spaghetti sauce

Olive oil, for the pan

1. Make the dairy-free cheese: Place all the ingredients in a food processor or high-speed blender and mix until the consistency is smooth, similar to a cheese sauce. Processing time will vary based on the power of your machine. Place the cheese in the refrigerator for at least 30 minutes. It will become solid and can be sliced like real cheese. Once it's solid, slice or grate the cheese.

2. Peel the plantains and cut them into thick slices. Place the plantain slices in a medium-sized pot and fill with water. Bring to a boil and continue to boil for 15 minutes.

3. While the plantains are boiling, cook the filling: Place the beef in a 12-inch skillet and turn the heat to medium. Season the beef with the salt and pepper and cook until the beef is no longer pink, about 6 minutes, stirring often to break up the meat.

4. Use a slotted spoon to transfer the beef to a bowl. Drain most of the excess fat from the skillet, leaving a little behind to cook the vegetables in. Place the onions, mushrooms, and garlic in the skillet and cook over medium heat for about 10 minutes, or until the onions are soft. Add to the cooked beef and set aside.

5. Once the plantains have finished boiling, drain the pot and place the plantains in a mixing bowl. Add the arrowroot starch, almond flour, and salt. Using a potato masher, mash together slowly until a dough forms. Then use your hands to work the dough for about 5 minutes. The dough should not be sticky. If it is, add up to 4 tablespoons more arrowroot starch, a tablespoon at a time, until it is no longer sticky. Divide the dough into three equal portions.

6. Preheat the oven to 375°F. Grease a 9-by-13-inch lasagna dish with olive oil.

7. Place a third of the dough between two sheets of wax paper. Using a rolling pin, roll the dough into a rectangle about 9 by 13 inches. Remove the top piece of wax paper and flip the dough, dough side down, into the dish, then remove the remaining sheet of wax paper. Remove any pieces of dough that do not fit and add them to areas that are bare.

8. Top the dough with half of the filling, half of the cheese, and one-third of the tomato sauce. Repeat with the second piece of dough (reusing the two sheets of wax paper to roll it out), remaining filling, and another third of the sauce.

9. Roll out the third piece of dough as described above and place on top of the second layer of filling. Spread the remaining cheese and sauce over it.

10. Cover with aluminum foil and bake for 45 minutes, then remove the foil and bake for an additional 15 minutes, or until the dough is cooked through in each layer. The cooked dough will resemble regular cooked dough in texture. Remove from the oven and allow the lasagna to cool for 10 minutes before slicing and serving.

CHAPTER 8

SIDES

Roasted
CAULIFLOWER

Yield: 4 servings   *Prep time:* 10 minutes   *Cook time:* 45 minutes

This is a simple but tasty recipe for roasted cauliflower. The nutritional yeast gives this dish a slightly cheesy flavor. I really like the taste and texture of coarse sea salt in this recipe, but you can use any type of sea salt you like.

1 medium head cauliflower (about 1¾ pounds), cored and cut into florets

¼ cup extra-virgin olive oil

¼ cup nutritional yeast

4 cloves garlic, finely chopped

2 teaspoons coarse sea salt

1. Preheat the oven to 425°F. Line two rimmed baking sheets with parchment paper.

2. In a large bowl, toss together all the ingredients until evenly coated.

3. Spread out the cauliflower on the two prepared baking sheets. Roast for 45 minutes, or until the cauliflower is golden in color and lightly toasted around the edges.

Loaded Mashed Cauliflower with
BACON & GREEN ONIONS

Yield: 4 servings   *Prep time:* 10 minutes   *Cook time:* 15 minutes

I am a huge fan of pureed cauliflower. I like it even more than the mashed potatoes it's often meant to replace. With this recipe, I took plain pureed cauliflower and kicked it up a notch by pairing it with bacon and green onions. You're going to love it!

1 medium head cauliflower (about 1¾ pounds), cored and chopped into 1-inch pieces

½ medium onion, chopped

¼ cup (½ stick) unsalted butter or ghee (page 56)

1 teaspoon fine sea salt

4 slices bacon, cooked and finely chopped

4 green onions, finely chopped

1. Place the cauliflower and onion in a 3-quart pot with enough water to cover and bring to a boil. Boil for 15 minutes, or until the cauliflower is tender. Drain the water from the pot.

2. Add the butter and salt to the cauliflower. Puree with a hand blender, or transfer the ingredients to a food processor and pulse until smooth.

3. Reserve some of the bacon and green onions for garnish and stir the rest into the cauliflower puree. Top with the reserved bacon and green onions and serve immediately.

Prosciutto-Wrapped
ASPARAGUS

Yield: 4 servings   *Prep time:* 15 minutes   *Cook time:* 25 minutes

My cousin once made a side dish for a family potluck that involved vegetables bundled together with prosciutto and cream cheese. It was a big hit. This is my dairy-free version, which has an added punch of flavor from fresh basil leaves. A whole prosciutto slice is too overpowering, so this recipe uses half a slice for every asparagus spear.

---

12 slices prosciutto

24 large fresh basil leaves

24 asparagus spears, trimmed

1 tablespoon ghee (page 56)

Fine sea salt and ground black pepper

1. Lay a slice of prosciutto on a cutting board with a long side facing you. Cut the slice in half diagonally, starting at one corner and ending at the opposite corner, to create two triangular pieces.

2. Place one basil leaf in the middle of a prosciutto slice. Place an asparagus spear along the long side of the prosciutto slice and roll the asparagus and prosciutto together. Gently set aside and repeat with the rest of the prosciutto slices, basil leaves, and asparagus spears.

3. Heat the ghee in a large skillet over medium-low heat. Place half of the wrapped asparagus pieces seam side down in the pan. Sprinkle lightly with salt and pepper and cook for 6 to 12 minutes, until the asparagus is crisp-tender and the prosciutto is crispy, turning once. Repeat with the rest of the asparagus pieces.

Savory Pureed
BUTTERNUT SQUASH

Yield: 4 servings   *Prep time:* 15 minutes   *Cook time:* 20 minutes

This pureed squash is reminiscent of autumn, and I love pairing it with savory dishes at that time of year. It's simple to make, but the herbs make it explode with flavor.

5 cups peeled and cubed butternut squash (1 small [1½- to 2-pound] squash)

¼ cup (½ stick) unsalted butter or ghee (page 56)

1 teaspoon onion powder

½ teaspoon fine sea salt

½ teaspoon dried rubbed sage

¼ teaspoon dried ground thyme

⅛ teaspoon ground black pepper

1. Place the butternut squash in a 3-quart pot and fill with enough water to cover the squash. Cover the pot and boil for 20 minutes, or until the squash is fork-tender. Drain the water from the pot.

2. Add the remaining ingredients to the pot with the squash. Puree with a hand blender, or transfer the ingredients to a food processor and pulse until smooth. Serve immediately.

Garlic-Roasted
CABBAGE

Yield: 4 servings   *Prep time:* 10 minutes   *Cook time:* 40 minutes

You might not believe it, but this recipe reminds me of garlic bread. The butter and garlic smothered all over the cabbage is amazing, and parts of the cabbage crisp up in the oven like chips. I could eat this dish all day long!

1 head purple or green cabbage (or ½ head each for color and variety), sliced from the top through the core into 1-inch-thick sections

2 cloves garlic

3 tablespoons unsalted butter or other fat of choice, melted

1½ teaspoons fine sea salt

1. Preheat the oven to 400°F. Line a rimmed baking sheet with parchment paper.

2. Place the cabbage slices on the prepared baking sheet. Cut one of the garlic cloves in half and rub the cut sides over the cabbage slices. Then chop the garlic halves and the other clove of garlic. Gently work the chopped garlic into the cabbage leaves with your fingers. Drizzle the melted butter all over the cabbage slices, then sprinkle with the salt.

3. Roast for 40 minutes, or until the cabbage is soft and the edges are crispy and lightly browned.

Cauliflower
RICE

Yield: 4 servings   *Prep time:* 10 minutes   *Cook time:* 5 minutes

Let me teach you how to make grain-free rice. Cauliflower is a perfect substitute for rice, and one of the bonuses is that it cooks faster! I use cauliflower rice in all my dishes that normally call for rice, such as fried rice.

1 medium head cauliflower (about 1¾ pounds)

2 tablespoons ghee (page 56)

½ teaspoon fine sea salt

1 tablespoon chopped fresh flat-leaf parsley, for garnish (optional)

1. Using a cheese grater or a food processor fitted with a grating attachment, grate the cauliflower to resemble rice.

2. Heat the ghee in a large skillet over medium heat. Add the cauliflower rice and sauté for 5 minutes, or until the texture is soft. While it is cooking, season it with the salt.

3. Garnish with parsley, if desired, and serve immediately.

Oven-Baked
SWEET POTATO FRIES

Yield: 4 servings   *Prep time:* 10 minutes   *Cook time:* 30 minutes

When I was stumped about what to use as a seasoning on my sweet potato fries, I reached out to a foodie friend in New Zealand and told her about my dilemma. She informed me that everyone in New Zealand uses chicken salt. "Chicken salt?" I repeated, not sure what she meant. She described it as a combination of spices, herbs, and chicken bouillon. This chicken salt was beginning to sound amazing! I used what I had on hand to create a chicken salt–inspired seasoning mixture, minus the bouillon.

4 sweet potatoes, peeled and sliced into ¼-inch strips

⅓ cup extra-virgin olive oil or preferred fat

2 teaspoons fine sea salt

1 teaspoon paprika

1 teaspoon onion powder

½ teaspoon dried parsley

½ teaspoon dried ground thyme

½ teaspoon ground black pepper

1. Preheat the oven to 450°F. Line a rimmed baking sheet with parchment paper.

2. Place the sweet potato strips in a large bowl. Add the olive oil and salt and toss until evenly coated.

3. Lay the sweet potato strips, without overlapping, on the prepared baking sheet. Bake for 30 minutes, or until the fries are soft on the inside and crisp on the outside, flipping halfway through.

4. Combine the seasonings in a small bowl. Sprinkle the mixture over the cooked fries, flipping them to make sure that they are evenly coated. Serve immediately.

Herb-Roasted
FINGERLING POTATOES

Yield: 4 servings   *Prep time:* 10 minutes   *Cook time:* 1 hour 20 minutes

Potatoes got a bad rap in the beginning of the Paleo movement because of their carb content. But behind the scenes, people were consuming them in their Paleo diets. One day, Hayley Mason and Bill Staley of *Primal Palate* posted a picture on their Facebook page with a potato on one side and a Paleo brownie on the other side and posed the question, "Why is one easily accepted as Paleo (the brownie) but not the humble potato in its unprocessed state?" Then the day came when Dallas and Melissa Hartwig of *Whole9* proclaimed the potato to be Paleo-approved. Sadly, the potato is still recovering from years of being on the blacklist. I hope this simple but delicious dish will erase any reservations you have about potatoes. You may even want seconds!

1½ pounds fingerling potatoes, halved lengthwise

¼ cup (½ stick) unsalted butter, melted, or preferred fat

1 tablespoon minced garlic

2 teaspoons dried parsley

1 teaspoon fine sea salt

1. Preheat the oven to 400°F. Line a rimmed baking sheet with parchment paper.

2. Place the potatoes in a large bowl with the melted butter, garlic, parsley, and salt. Toss until evenly coated. Spread the potatoes, without overlapping, on the prepared baking sheet.

3. Bake for 1 hour 20 minutes, or until the potatoes are soft on the inside and crispy on the outside, flipping once halfway through cooking. Serve immediately.

Crispy Sautéed Kale with
BACON & ONIONS

Yield: 4 servings   *Prep time:* 10 minutes   *Cook time:* 15 minutes

I love cooking kale until it's crunchy like kale chips. It makes me feel like I'm eating chips with my dinner. Other than eating raw kale in a salad, this is the only way I like it. If you prefer your kale softer, sauté it just until tender.

---

4 slices bacon, chopped

1½ pounds kale, tough stems removed, rinsed, dried, and chopped

1 large onion, diced

Fine sea salt and ground black pepper

1. In a large skillet, cook the bacon over medium heat until crisp. Remove with a slotted spoon.

2. Add the kale and onion to the skillet and stir to coat in the bacon fat. Cook, stirring frequently, until the kale is crispy, about 7 minutes.

3. Return the bacon to the pan and season with salt and pepper. Serve immediately.

Mashed Banana
SWEET POTATOES

Yield: 6 servings Prep time: 15 minutes Cook time: 1 hour

I first ate this amazing dish in Mexico. It combines mashed sweet potatoes with bananas to create a heavenly flavor. I loved the sweetness that the bananas added and knew I had to re-create it at home immediately. Roasting the potatoes and bananas brings a depth of flavor to this dish.

8 ripe bananas, peeled and cut into 1-inch-thick pieces

4 large sweet potatoes, peeled and diced

2 cups (4 sticks) unsalted butter, divided

Fine sea salt

1. Preheat the oven to 400°F. Line a rimmed baking sheet with parchment paper.

2. Spread the bananas and sweet potatoes on the prepared baking sheet. Cut ¼ cup (½ stick) of the butter into small cubes and randomly place them among the potatoes and bananas.

3. Roast for 1 hour, or until the sweet potatoes are fork-tender.

4. Place the roasted sweet potatoes and bananas in a 5-quart mixing bowl. Add the remaining 1¾ cups (3½ sticks) of butter and season with salt. Puree with a hand blender, or transfer the ingredients to a food processor and pulse until smooth.

Roasted Carrots
WITH A KICK

Yield: 4 servings *Prep time:* 10 minutes *Cook time:* 45 minutes

These carrots have a little kick to them from the Tabasco sauce. They're a nice change from the boiled carrots I grew up with.

8 large carrots, peeled and cut into 1-inch pieces

¼ cup extra-virgin olive oil

½ teaspoon garlic powder

½ teaspoon paprika

½ teaspoon onion powder

1 teaspoon fine sea salt

½ teaspoon Tabasco pepper sauce

1. Preheat the oven to 400°F. Line a rimmed baking sheet with parchment paper.

2. In a large bowl, toss together all the ingredients until evenly coated. Spread out the carrots on the prepared baking sheet.

3. Roast for 45 minutes, or until the carrots are fork-tender and lightly toasted around the edges, flipping halfway through.

SIDES Sides SIDES SIDES Sides SIDES SIDES Sides SIDES SIDES Sides SIDES

Roasted
LEEKS

Yield: 4 servings   *Prep time:* 5 minutes   *Cook time:* 45 minutes

I was having a casual dinner at a friend's apartment, and we were trying to figure out what to cook for dinner. She wanted to try roasting some greens to go with our main dish, and she only had leeks. The idea of roasted leeks sounded unappealing to me, but I decided to give it a try. We cut up some leeks, sprinkled them with olive oil and salt, and roasted them to perfection. Oh, my! I love roasted leeks now. I can't remember my life before them.

4 leeks, washed, halved lengthwise, and washed again

¼ cup extra-virgin olive oil

Fine sea salt

1. Preheat the oven to 375°F. Have on hand a large baking dish.

2. Dry the leeks well. If needed to fit them in the baking dish, cut them in half crosswise. Pour the olive oil over the leeks and sprinkle generously with salt.

3. Bake for 45 minutes, or until the leeks are slightly browned and tender when pierced with a knife.

DESSERTS

Birthday CAKE

Yield: One 2-layer, 8-inch cake (10 servings)   *Prep time:* 15 minutes, plus 5 minutes for the icing
Cook time: 35 minutes

This is my favorite recipe for a classic vanilla cake that is perfect for birthdays and family gatherings. You can switch out the strawberries in the middle with any fresh fruit you have on hand.

FOR THE BATTER:

1½ cups sifted coconut flour

¼ cup arrowroot starch

1 teaspoon baking soda

½ teaspoon fine sea salt

16 large eggs, separated

½ cup maple syrup

1 tablespoon plus 1 teaspoon cream of tartar

1 cup coconut oil

1 tablespoon vanilla extract

FOR THE FILLING:

8 strawberries, halved

1 recipe Basic Cupcake Icing (page 78)

½ cup blueberries, for garnish (optional)

½ cup halved strawberries, for garnish (optional)

1. Preheat the oven to 350°F. Line the bottoms of two 8-inch round cake pans with parchment paper and grease the sides of the pans.

2. In a bowl, whisk together the coconut flour, arrowroot starch, baking soda, and salt. Set aside.

3. In a large metal or glass bowl, using a hand mixer on low speed, combine the egg whites, maple syrup, and cream of tartar. Increase the speed to high and whip the mixture until stiff peaks form.

4. In a separate bowl, using the hand mixer on medium speed, cream the egg yolks, coconut oil, and vanilla until smooth. Add the coconut flour mixture to the egg yolk mixture and mix on medium speed until smooth.

5. With the mixer running on low speed, slowly add the egg yolk and flour mixture to the whipped egg whites.

6. Divide the batter between the two prepared pans and smooth out the tops. Bake for 30 to 35 minutes, until the tops are firm to the touch and a toothpick inserted in the middle of the cakes comes out clean. Transfer the pans to a wire rack and let the cakes cool completely in the pans.

7. When the cake layers are completely cool, assemble the cake: Run a knife around the edges of the pans to loosen the cakes. Invert one of the cake layers onto a cake stand. Peel off the parchment paper. Spread half of the icing on top of the cake, then add the halved strawberries for the filling. Top with the second cake layer and remove the parchment. Spread the remaining icing on the top of the cake.

8. Garnish with blueberries and halved strawberries, if desired. Consume the cake within 2 days. Store covered in refrigerator.

Chocolate CAKE

Yield: One 2-layer, 8-inch cake (10 servings)   *Prep time:* 10 minutes   *Cook time:* 45 minutes

Everyone needs a classic chocolate cake in their recipe box. My version is truly flourless, relying on cocoa powder to act as the flour. I designed this cake to be fudgy and dense in texture rather than light and fluffy. It's like a cross between a brownie and cake!

FOR THE BATTER:

8 large eggs

2 cups unsweetened cocoa powder

2 cups coconut palm sugar

1 cup coconut oil

1 tablespoon vanilla extract

2 teaspoons cream of tartar

½ teaspoon baking soda

½ teaspoon fine sea salt

FOR THE ICING (MAKES 3 CUPS):

8 ounces bittersweet baking chocolate, roughly chopped

1 cup full-fat coconut milk

1 cup coconut palm sugar

1 cup palm shortening

1. Preheat the oven to 350°F. Line the bottoms of two 8-inch round cake pans with parchment paper and grease the sides of the pans.

2. In a large bowl, using a hand mixer, mix together the eggs, cocoa powder, coconut palm sugar, coconut oil, vanilla, and cream of tartar until combined. Add the baking soda and salt (these are added last to avoid activating the baking soda too early) and mix until combined.

3. Divide the batter between the two pans and smooth out the tops.

4. Bake for 40 to 45 minutes, until the tops are firm to the touch and a toothpick inserted in the middle of the cakes comes out clean. Place the pans on a wire rack and let the cakes cool completely in the pans.

5. While the cakes are baking, make the icing: Place the chocolate in a medium-sized saucepan. Turn the heat to medium-low and stir constantly until the chocolate has melted, about 7 minutes. Set the chocolate aside to cool for 10 minutes.

6. Place the rest of the ingredients for the icing in a mixing bowl and, using the hand mixer on high speed, beat until the icing is light and fluffy, about 5 minutes.

7. Once the chocolate has cooled, slowly drizzle it into the icing while the mixer is running on high speed. Beat for 5 minutes. Set the icing aside.

8. When the cake layers are completely cool, assemble the cake: Run a knife around the edges of the pans to loosen the cakes. Invert one of the cake layers onto a cake stand. Peel off the parchment paper. Spread about one-third of the icing on the top of the cake, then top with the second cake layer. Remove the parchment from the top cake layer and spread the rest of the icing over the whole cake.

Note: The icing can be made up to 3 days in advance and stored in the refrigerator. If using the icing after it has been refrigerated, place it in a bowl and beat with a hand mixer until light and fluffy.

Carrot Cake
CUPCAKES

Yield: 20 cupcakes   *Prep time:* 10 minutes, plus 5 minutes for the icing   *Cook time:* 20 minutes

I love these cupcakes. They actually taste best the next day, when their flavor has deepened. For baked goods that contain a lot of wet ingredients, such as carrots and pineapple, I prefer to use almond flour, which is not as sensitive as coconut flour to slight changes in the amount of liquid. Carrot cake traditionally has a cream cheese icing, but here the Basic Cupcake Icing (page 78) uses palm shortening to create a light, creamy, dairy-free icing.

2¼ cups almond flour

1 cup coconut palm sugar

¼ cup arrowroot starch

1 tablespoon ground cinnamon, plus more for garnish (optional)

2 teaspoons cream of tartar

1 teaspoon baking soda

½ teaspoon fine sea salt

½ teaspoon ginger powder

¼ teaspoon ground nutmeg

6 large eggs

2 tablespoons coconut oil, melted but not hot

1½ cups peeled and grated carrots

1 cup golden raisins

2 recipes Basic Cupcake Icing (page 78)

1. Preheat the oven to 350°F. Line two 12-well muffin pans with 20 muffin liners.

2. In a large bowl, thoroughly whisk together the almond flour, coconut palm sugar, arrowroot starch, cinnamon, cream of tartar, baking soda, salt, ginger powder, and nutmeg.

3. In a separate bowl, whisk together the eggs and coconut oil until smooth. Add the wet ingredients to the dry ingredients and mix together. Stir in the carrots and raisins.

4. Spoon the batter into the lined muffin cups, filling each three-quarters of the way full.

5. Bake for 20 minutes, or until the tops are firm to the touch and a toothpick inserted in the middle of a cupcake comes out clean.

6. Transfer the cupcakes to a wire rack and allow to cool completely.

7. Pipe the icing onto the cooled cupcakes. Sprinkle some cinnamon on top, if desired.

8. Store the cupcakes in an airtight container at room temperature for up to 2 days.

Caramel
CHOCOLATE NUT BARS

Yield: 16 squares   *Prep time:* 5 minutes, plus at least 4 hours to chill
Cook time: 15 minutes, plus 35 minutes for the sauces

This flavor combo was inspired by the classic Turtles Caramel Nut Clusters. Technically it's a millionaire's shortbread recipe with whole pecans snuggled into the caramel. The caramel in this recipe is thick and hardens slightly, making it ideal for this treat. If you need to make these nut-free, replace the base used here with Coconut Flour Bar Base (page 84) and omit the pecans.

FOR THE BASE:

2 cups almond flour

¼ cup coconut oil, melted but not hot

¼ cup coconut palm sugar

1 large egg

⅛ teaspoon fine sea salt

1 recipe Caramel Sauce (page 82)

½ cup raw pecans

1 recipe Chocolate Sauce (page 80)

1. Preheat the oven to 350°F. Line the bottom of an 8-inch square baking pan with parchment paper and grease the sides of the pan.

2. Make the base: In a large bowl, combine the almond flour, coconut oil, coconut palm sugar, egg, and salt. Evenly press the dough into the bottom of the prepared baking pan.

3. Bake for 15 minutes, or until the crust is lightly brown and firm to the touch. Gently sweep away any crumbs.

4. Spread the caramel sauce over the baked crust. Sprinkle the pecans over the caramel. Allow to cool, then spread the chocolate sauce on top. Refrigerate until firm, at least 4 hours or overnight.

5. Cut into 16 squares. Store in the refrigerator.

BROWNIES

Yield: 16 brownies   *Prep time:* 10 minutes   *Cook time:* 35 minutes

These brownies are dense, fudgy, and grain-free. Score! I aim to please with this recipe. The brownies are quick to assemble, but you need to be patient and allow them to fully cool before sneaking a bite.

1 cup coconut palm sugar

½ cup almond flour

½ teaspoon fine sea salt

4 large eggs

1 teaspoon vanilla extract

1¼ cups semi-sweet chocolate chips

¾ cup coconut oil

1. Preheat the oven to 350°F. Line the bottom and sides of an 8-inch square baking pan with parchment paper, leaving 2 inches of overhang.

2. Place the coconut palm sugar, almond flour, salt, eggs, and vanilla in the bowl of a stand mixer fitted with the whisk attachment. With the mixer on medium speed, mix together the ingredients until combined. Alternatively, combine in a large bowl and whisk by hand.

3. Put an inch of water in the bottom of a double boiler and the chocolate chips and coconut oil in the top. If you don't have a double boiler, you can place a heatproof glass or metal bowl over a pot filled with 1 inch of water. Over medium-low heat, melt the chocolate chips and coconut oil, stirring constantly, about 5 minutes. Once melted and smooth, remove from the heat to cool slightly.

4. With the stand mixer (or a hand mixer) running on medium speed, pour the chocolate mixture into the almond flour mixture and mix until fully combined.

5. Pour the batter into the prepared pan and smooth the top. Bake until the top begins to firm up and a toothpick inserted into the center comes out with a few moist crumbs attached, about 30 minutes.

6. Transfer the pan to a wire rack and let the brownies cool completely in the pan. Once cool, lift the brownies out of the pan using the overhanging parchment paper and transfer to a cutting board. Cut into 16 squares.

7. Store the brownies in an airtight container at room temperature for up to 4 days.

Cinnamon
BUNS

Yield: 9 buns   *Prep time:* 15 minutes, plus 15 minutes to chill the dough
Cook time: 35 minutes, plus 5 minutes for the icing

Some people consider cinnamon buns a breakfast food, but to me they are dessert and definitely an occasional treat! My healthier, Paleo-friendly cinnamon buns have a satisfying, slightly dense texture and are definitely less sweet than the typical version, but they're still an indulgence.

1¾ cups almond flour

1½ cups tapioca starch, plus more for rolling out the dough

1 cup potato starch

½ cup cane sugar

1 tablespoon instant yeast (see Note, page 256)

1 teaspoon cream of tartar

½ teaspoon baking soda

½ teaspoon fine sea salt

4 large eggs

¼ cup coconut oil, melted, plus more for the pan

FOR THE FILLING:

¼ cup plus 2 tablespoons coconut oil, softened

½ cup coconut palm sugar

2 tablespoons ground cinnamon

1 recipe Basic Cupcake Icing (page 78)

1. Preheat oven to 350°F. Grease the bottom of an 8-inch square baking pan with coconut oil.

2. In a large bowl, thoroughly whisk together the almond flour, tapioca starch, potato starch, cane sugar, instant yeast, cream of tartar, baking soda, and salt.

3. In a separate bowl, mix together the eggs and melted coconut oil, then add the wet ingredients to the dry ingredients. Mix together using a hand mixer on medium speed until a sticky dough forms, about 2 minutes.

4. Place the bowl of dough in the freezer for 15 minutes. This will make the dough firm enough to work with.

5. Place a large piece of parchment paper (about 20 inches long) on a work surface and sprinkle a generous amount of tapioca starch all over it. Transfer the dough to the parchment paper. Sprinkle some tapioca starch on top of the dough and on a rolling pin to prevent sticking. Roll into an 18-by-8-inch rectangle.

6. In a small bowl, mix together the ingredients for the filling and then spread it over the dough to the edges.

7. Using a knife or pizza cutter, cut the dough crosswise into 9 strips, each 2 inches wide by 8 inches long.

8. Starting at the short end, roll up each cinnamon bun. Gently place the buns, cut side up, in the prepared baking pan, arranging them three to a row, spaced apart. The buns will expand as they bake.

9. Bake for 35 minutes, or until a toothpick inserted into the center of one of the buns comes out clean.

10. Allow the buns to cool, then top them with the icing. Store in an airtight container at room temperature for up to 3 days.

Apple

CRUMBLE

Yield: 6 servings   *Prep time:* 10 minutes   *Cook time:* 1 hour

At first I was going to share a recipe for classic apple pie with you, and then I decided to make an apple pie with a crumb topping, but then I decided that I prefer an even easier but equally delicious crustless version, thus this recipe. The topping is inspired by a Paleo granola that I make. It's sweet and crunchy and pairs beautifully with the soft, warm apples, and you can make it extremely quickly.

FOR THE CRUMBLE TOPPING:

1 cup sliced almonds

1 cup chopped walnuts

1 cup unsweetened coconut flakes

¼ cup maple syrup

2 teaspoons ground cinnamon

¼ teaspoon fine sea salt

FOR THE FILLING:

7 medium McIntosh apples, peeled, cored, and cut into ½-inch slices (about 7 cups)

¼ cup plus 2 tablespoons coconut palm sugar

2 tablespoons arrowroot starch

2 teaspoons ground cinnamon

¼ teaspoon ground nutmeg

¼ teaspoon fine sea salt

1. Preheat the oven to 350°F.

2. In a large bowl, mix together all the topping ingredients and set aside.

3. In another large bowl, mix together all the filling ingredients and pour into an 8-inch pie dish, making sure to level the mixture.

4. Evenly spread the crumble topping over the apple filling.

5. Cover with aluminum foil and bake for 45 minutes, then remove the foil and bake for another 15 minutes, or until the apples are soft and the topping is lightly toasted.

6. Serve warm. Store leftovers in the refrigerator for up to 4 days.

Chocolate-Dipped
HONEYCOMB

Yield: 6 servings   *Prep time:* 5 minutes, plus 30 minutes for the honeycomb to harden
Cook time: 12 minutes

This dessert is extremely easy to make. You might be shaking your head at an all-sugar dessert recipe in a Paleo cookbook, but hear me out. This recipe makes enough candy for six people or more, which means that each serving contains less than 2 tablespoons of sugar without the chocolate coating.

By the way, I am all for getting kids involved in cooking and baking, but this is one recipe that I recommend only grown-ups make. The hot sugar will burn you if you happen to drop some on your skin.

½ cup cane sugar

3 tablespoons raw honey

2 tablespoons water

1 teaspoon baking soda

3 cups semi-sweet chocolate chips

1. Combine the sugar, honey, and water in a heavy-bottomed 2-quart saucepan. Without turning on the heat, stir the ingredients together.

2. Place a candy thermometer in the pan. Turn the heat to medium-high and do not stir again. Cook until the mixture reaches 300°F and turns a light amber color, about 7 minutes. If the sugar starts to burn in one area, rotate the pan, but do not stir the ingredients.

3. While the sugar mixture is cooking, line a 9-by-13-inch pan with parchment paper.

4. When the sugar mixture reaches 300°F, remove the pan from the heat and quickly stir in the baking soda. Do not overstir, which will result in a flat end product. The mixture will expand rapidly.

5. Pour the mixture into the prepared pan; do not use a spatula to move it around. Allow the honeycomb to harden for at least 30 minutes.

6. Once cool, gently break apart the honeycomb into smaller pieces.

7. Line a rimmed baking sheet with parchment paper.

8. Put an inch of water in the bottom of a double boiler and the chocolate chips in the top. If you don't have a double boiler, you can place a heatproof glass or metal bowl over a pot filled with 1 inch of water. Over medium-low heat, melt the chocolate chips, stirring constantly, about 5 minutes.

9. Dip the honeycomb pieces into the chocolate and lay the dipped honeycomb on the prepared baking sheet. Allow the chocolate coating to harden, about 30 minutes. (If you wish, place the baking sheet in the fridge to speed up the hardening process to about 10 minutes.)

10. Store the honeycomb in an airtight container at room temperature for up to 4 days.

Dad's N' Oatmeal COOKIES

Yield: 14 cookies   *Prep time:* 5 minutes   *Cook time:* 10 minutes

While I was growing up, my dad usually had his own box of store-bought oatmeal cookies that he kept hidden from my brothers and me. I have re-created them here with a grain-free twist. Coconut flakes replace oatmeal, which is naturally gluten-free but is contaminated with gluten during processing. The spices in these cookies make them irresistible. You might consider hiding them, too!

1 cup almond flour

1 cup unsweetened shredded coconut

¾ cup coconut palm sugar

¼ cup arrowroot starch

¼ cup coconut oil, melted

2 large eggs

1½ teaspoons ground cinnamon

1 teaspoon vanilla extract

½ teaspoon fine sea salt

½ teaspoon ground ginger

¼ teaspoon ground nutmeg

1. Preheat the oven to 350°F. Line a cookie sheet with parchment paper.

2. Mix all the ingredients together in a medium-sized bowl. Form the dough into 1-inch balls.

3. Place the dough balls on the prepared baking sheet, spacing them 2 inches apart, and flatten to ¼ inch thick with the palm of your hand.

4. Bake for 8 to 10 minutes, until the edges are brown and the centers are firm. Transfer the cookies to a wire rack and let cool completely.

5. Store the cookies in an airtight container at room temperature for up to 4 days, or in the freezer for up to 3 months.

Chocolate Chip
COOKIES

Yield: 16 cookies   *Prep time:* 10 minutes   *Cook time:* 20 minutes

I bet you can't stop at just one of these cookies! I find them utterly irresistible. They're sweet but not too sweet and crisp on the outside but soft on the inside. Like all great cookies, these taste fantastic just out of the oven.

1 cup almond flour

¼ cup arrowroot starch

½ teaspoon baking soda

½ teaspoon fine sea salt

½ cup coconut palm sugar

¼ cup coconut oil

1 large egg

1 teaspoon vanilla extract

1 cup semi-sweet chocolate chips

1. Preheat the oven to 350°F. Line two cookie sheets with parchment paper.

2. In a small bowl, thoroughly whisk together the almond flour, arrowroot starch, baking soda, and salt.

3. In a large bowl, using a hand mixer on medium speed, beat the coconut palm sugar, coconut oil, egg, and vanilla until smooth, about 2 minutes. Slowly add the flour mixture and mix just until incorporated. Use a spatula to stir in the chocolate chips.

4. Using two soup spoons, drop the dough in roughly 1-inch portions, spaced 2 inches apart, onto the prepared cookie sheets.

5. Bake, one sheet at a time, for 8 to 10 minutes, until the bottoms and edges of the cookies are lightly browned and the tops feel firm when gently touched. Let cool on the cookie sheet for at least 1 minute, then transfer the cookies to a wire rack to cool completely.

6. Store in an airtight container at room temperature for up to 4 days, or in the freezer for up to 3 months.

Strawberry Swirl
ICE CREAM

Yield: 1 pint *Prep time:* 10 minutes, plus about 20 minutes to churn

Coconut cream makes a great base for dairy-free ice cream. I also use a large number of egg yolks to create a scoopable, creamy ice cream. Keep in mind, though, that the egg yolks aren't cooked in this recipe, so salmonella may be a risk (and it's more of a concern for pregnant women and kids). Using high-quality pastured eggs may reduce the risk, but it's not a guarantee. Ice cream made with pastured egg yolks has a yellow appearance. Any fruit can be used in place of the strawberries.

FOR THE STRAWBERRY PUREE:

1½ cups pureed strawberries (about 3 cups whole strawberries)

1 tablespoon maple syrup

2 teaspoons arrowroot starch

½ teaspoon fresh lemon juice

FOR THE BASE:

2¼ cups coconut cream (see page 33)

6 large egg yolks

½ cup maple syrup

2 teaspoons raw apple cider vinegar

2 teaspoons vanilla extract

1. Make the strawberry puree first: Mix together all the puree ingredients and set aside.

2. Make the ice cream base: Place the coconut cream, egg yolks, maple syrup, vinegar, and vanilla in a large bowl and, using a whisk, mix until incorporated.

3. Turn on your ice cream maker and pour in the ice cream base. Churn until the mixture resembles soft-serve ice cream, about 20 minutes, depending on the machine.

4. Scoop the ice cream into a container. Drizzle the strawberry puree into the ice cream and swirl it around.

5. Freeze for at least 2 hours, or consume immediately. Once stored in the freezer, homemade ice cream tends to be harder than store-bought ice cream. Allow 10 minutes for it to soften before scooping.

Special equipment:

Ice cream maker (see Note)

Note: Follow the directions for your ice cream maker and remember to place the insulated ice cream container in the freezer 24 hours beforehand, if required.

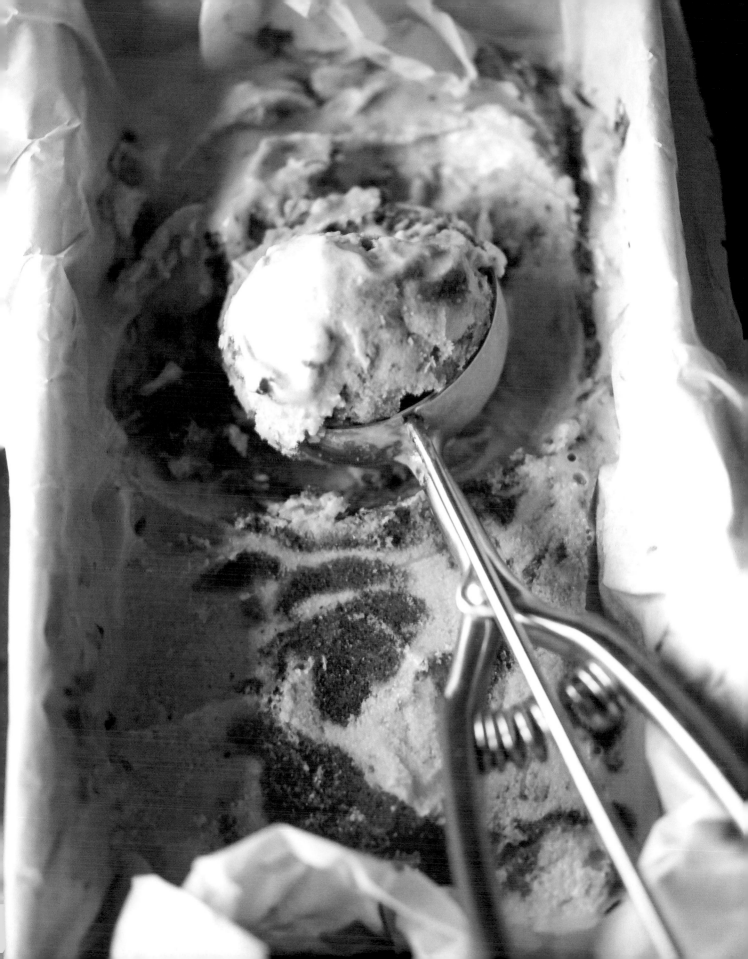

Chocolate Truffle Custard with
SALTED CASHEW CRUST

Yield: 8 servings *Prep time:* 15 minutes *Cook time:* 40 minutes, plus 8 hours to chill

Every birthday for the past ten years, my brother Mark has asked my mom to make him a decadent chocolate truffle cheesecake. It gets rave reviews. I've made a dairy-free version using custard in place of the cream-cheese-and-sour-cream base and paired it with a salted cashew crust. The original version has a lovely tart taste that I've replicated here with lemon juice.

FOR THE CRUST:

2 cups raw cashews

16 Medjool dates, pitted

½ teaspoon fine sea salt

FOR THE FILLING:

½ cup semi-sweet chocolate chips

8 large egg yolks

1 cup full-fat coconut milk

½ cup maple syrup

¼ cup fresh lemon juice

1 teaspoon vanilla extract

⅛ teaspoon fine sea salt

1. Preheat the oven to 325°F.

2. Make the crust: Place the cashews, dates, and salt in a food processor. Pulse at least six times to achieve a mixture that sticks together.

3. Place the crust mixture in a 9-inch springform pan. Cover with a sheet of wax paper and press the mixture into the bottom of the pan, building it 1 inch up the sides. Discard the wax paper.

4. Make the filling: Put an inch of water in the bottom of a double boiler and the chocolate chips in the top. If you don't have a double boiler, you can place a heatproof glass or metal bowl over a pot filled with 1 inch of water. Over medium-low heat, melt the chocolate chips, stirring constantly, about 5 minutes. Set aside.

5. Place the remaining filling ingredients in a large bowl. Using a hand mixer on medium speed, mix until combined. With the mixer running on low speed, drizzle in the melted chocolate.

6. Pour the mixture over the crust. Bake for 30 to 35 minutes, until the custard is firm around the edges and jiggles slightly in the center.

7. Remove from the oven and let cool to room temperature in the pan, then cover and refrigerate overnight.

8. Carefully run a knife around the inside edge of the pan to loosen the crust, then release the ring. Slice into 8 servings.

9. Store covered in the refrigerator for up to 4 days.

Thank You

I want to thank Victory Belt for giving me this opportunity to write a cookbook that I hope will inspire people for generations. I want to especially thank Erich Krauss, Michele Farrington, Holly Jennings, and Susan Lloyd.

Thank you, Caitlin Weeks and Nabil Boumrar, for providing a writing sanctuary for me in Nashville. Thank you, Caitlin, for being there every step of the way—from helping me pick out props and taking photos at the farmers' markets to the endless rounds of grocery shopping, you never complained and you always encouraged me.

Thank you, Karen Sorenson, for always being there when I needed to brainstorm recipe ideas and for helping me get through many cookbook meltdowns.

Thank you, Diane Sanfilippo, for submitting my first digital cookbook, *Indulge*, to Victory Belt and for always encouraging me. Your words of encouragement on my latest cookbook work always brightened my day and made me feel like I can do this!

Thank you, Spruce Lee Lovett, for your unconditional love and cuddles while I moved you three times during the writing of this cookbook.

Thank you, Lydia Shatney, Marie Houlden, and Natcha Maithai, for helping me learn how to heal my body.

Thank you, Jennifer Robins, for being a friend I could lean on during the writing of this cookbook.

Thank you, Stephanie Gaudreau, for your amazing photography tips and encouragement.

Thank you, Kristen Parkhill, for pre-editing my work before I handed it in to Victory Belt and for trying my recipes.

Thank you, Daniel and Heather Dessinger and kids, for allowing me to photograph your farm and being such loving and supportive friends. Most of all, thank you, Heather, for writing such a beautiful, thoughtful foreword.

Thank you, Betty Johnston, for allowing me to use your cottage to finish creating and photographing the recipes.

Thank you, Katie Goudie, Marilee Barlow, and Kelly Matsudaira, for helping with administrative duties on the blog.

Thank you, Louise Hendon, Heather Katsonga-Woodward, and Julia Roy, Arsy Vartanian, Jessica Bennett Espinoza, Kate Doubler, Kelly Bejelly, Orleatha Smith, Sylvie McCracken, and Vivica Menegaz, for all your advice during our mastermind sessions.

Thank you, Sheila Walsh Dunton, for being a friend to lean on and always educating me on how to eat to nurture my body.

Thank you, Mom and Dad, for all the help you provided while I wrote the cookbook. Thank you for putting up with the constantly messy kitchen.

Resource GUIDE

PASTURED MEATS AND ORGANIC FRUITS AND VEGETABLES

Eat Wild (www.eatwild.com): Find farmers in your area who sell grass-fed meats and other products.

Local Harvest (www.localharvest.org): Locate CSAs, farmers' markets, and small farms in your area.

US Wellness Meats (www.grasslandbeef.com): If there are no farmers or butchers in your area that offer grass-fed beef, pastured pork, or free-range chicken, you can purchase them online here.

PANTRY

Below is a list of my preferred brands of various pantry items. To learn more about them, visit their sites. Many of these products can be found at grocery stores; all can be purchased from online discount retailers such as Amazon or Vitacost.com, and in many cases directly from the brand's site.

Artisana (www.artisanafoods.com): Coconut butter

Barney Butter (www.barneybutter.com): Barney's almond butter

Bob's Red Mill (www.bobsredmill.com): Almond meal, arrowroot starch, coconut flour, and tapioca flour

Bragg (www.bragg.com): Apple cider vinegar

Coconut Secret (www.coconutsecret.com): Coconut aminos

Enjoy Life (www.enjoylifefoods.com): Dairy-free chocolate chips

Fatworks Foods (www.fatworksfoods.com): Lard, duck fat, and tallow

Great Lakes (www.greatlakesgelatin.com): Grass-fed beef gelatin

Honeyville (www.honeyville.com): Blanched, superfine almond flour

Kerrygold (www.kerrygold.com): Grass-fed butter

Kombucha Kamp (www.kombuchakamp.com): SCOBYs and kombucha-brewing supplies

Natural Value (www.naturalvalue.com): Coconut milk

Nutiva (www.nutiva.com): Coconut flour and organic virgin coconut oil

Red Boat Fish Sauce (www.redboatfishsauce.com): Fish sauce

Red Star Yeast (www.redstaryeast.com): Yeast

Tropical Traditions (www.tropicaltraditions.com): Coconut flour, gold label virgin coconut oil, virgin palm oil, and raw honey

SPECIALTY KITCHEN TOOLS

Paderno (www.paderno.com): Spiral slicer

Further READING

THOUGHT-PROVOKING BOOKS

Ballantyne, Sarah. *The Paleo Approach: Reverse Autoimmune Disease and Heal Your Body.* Las Vegas: Victory Belt Publishing, 2013.

Durant, John. *The Paleo Manifesto: Ancient Wisdom for Lifelong Health.* New York: Harmony Books, 2013.

Fallon, Sally, with Mary Enig. *Nourishing Traditions: The Cookbook That Challenges Politically Correct Nutrition and the Diet Dictocrats,* rev. 2nd ed. Washington, DC: NewTrends Publishing, 2003.

Jaminet, Paul, and Shou-Ching Jaminet. *Perfect Health Diet: Regain Health and Lose Weight by Eating the Way You Were Meant to Eat.* New York: Scribner, 2013.

Michaelis, Kristen. *Beautiful Babies: Nutrition for Fertility, Pregnancy, Breastfeeding, & Baby's First Foods.* Las Vegas: Victory Belt Publishing, 2013.

Price, Weston A. *Nutrition and Physical Degeneration,* 8th ed. Price-Pottenger Nutrition Foundation, 2008.

Sanfilippo, Diane. *Practical Paleo: A Customized Approach to Health and a Whole-Foods Lifestyle.* Las Vegas: Victory Belt Publishing, 2012.

Sisson, Mark. *The Primal Blueprint: Reprogram Your Genes for Effortless Weight Loss, Vibrant Health, and Boundless Energy.* Malibu, CA: Primal Blueprint Publishing, 2013.

Standage, Tom. *An Edible History of Humanity.* New York: Walker & Company, 2010.

Wahls, Terry. *The Wahls Protocol: A Radical New Way to Treat All Chronic Autoimmune Conditions Using Paleo Principles.* New York: Avery, 2014.

Wolf, Robb. *The Paleo Solution: The Original Human Diet.* Las Vegas: Victory Belt Publishing, 2010.

GENERAL PALEO COOKBOOKS

Bauer, Juli, and George Byrant. *The Paleo Kitchen: Finding Primal Joy in Modern Cooking.* Las Vegas: Victory Belt Publishing, 2014.

Bejelly, Kelly. *Paleo Eats: 111 Comforting Gluten-Free, Grain-Free and Dairy-Free Recipes for the Foodie in You.* Las Vegas: Victory Belt Publishing, 2014.

Gaudreau, Stephanie. *The Performance Paleo Cookbook: Recipes for Training Harder, Getting Stronger and Gaining the Competitive Edge.* Salem, MA: Page Street Publishing, 2015.

Hannah, Ciarra. *The Frugal Paleo Cookbook: Affordable, Easy & Delicious Paleo Cooking.* Salem, MA: Page Street Publishing, 2014.

Joulwan, Melissa. *Well Fed: Paleo Recipes for People Who Love to Eat,* 2nd ed. Austin, TX: Smudge Publishing, 2011.

DITCH THE WHEAT

Mason, Hayley, and Bill Staley. *Make it Paleo II: Over 175 New Grain-Free Recipes for the Primal Palate.* Las Vegas: Victory Belt Publishing, 2015.

Tam, Michelle, and Henry Fong. *Nom Nom Paleo: Food for Humans.* Kansas City: Andrews McMeel Publishing, 2013.

Toth, Stacy, and Matthew McCarry. *Beyond Bacon: Paleo Recipes that Respect the Whole Hog.* Las Vegas: Victory Belt Publishing, 2013.

Vitt, Carrie. *The Grain-Free Family Table: 125 Delicious Recipes for Fresh, Healthy Eating Every Day.* New York: William Morrow Cookbooks, 2014.

Walker, Danielle. *Against All Grain: Delectable Paleo Recipes to Eat Well and Feel Great.* Las Vegas: Victory Belt Publishing, 2013.

Weeks, Caitlin, Nabil Boumrar, and Diane Sanfilippo. *Mediterranean Paleo Cooking: Over 150 Fresh Coastal Recipes for a Relaxed, Gluten-Free Lifestyle.* Las Vegas: Victory Belt Publishing, 2014.

Weissman, Joshua. *The Slim Palate Paleo Cookbook.* Las Vegas: Victory Belt Publishing, 2014.

PALEO BAKING COOKBOOKS

Angell, Brittany. *Every Last Crumb: Paleo Bread and Beyond.* Las Vegas: Victory Belt Publishing, 2014.

Barajas, Vanessa. *Clean Eating with a Dirty Mind: Over 150 Paleo-Inspired Recipes for Every Craving.* Las Vegas: Victory Belt Publishing, 2015.

Hulet, Jenni. *My Paleo Patisserie: An Artisan Approach to Grain-Free Baking.* Las Vegas: Victory Belt Publishing, 2015.

Smith, Kelly. *Everyday Grain-Free Baking: Over 100 Recipes for Deliciously Easy Grain-Free and Gluten-Free Baking.* Avon, MA: Adams Media, 2015.

AUTOIMMUNE PALEO COOKBOOKS

Alt, Angie, with Jenifer Beehler. *The Alternative Autoimmune Cookbook: Eating for All Phases of the Paleo Autoimmune Protocol.* 2014.

Ballantyne, Sarah. *The Paleo Approach: Reverse Autoimmune Disease and Heal Your Body.* Las Vegas: Victory Belt Publishing, 2013.

Bryant, Rachael. *Nourish: The Paleo Healing Cookbook: Easy Yet Flavorful Recipes that Fight Autoimmune Illnesses.* Salem, MA: Page Street Publishing, 2015.

Trescott, Mickey. *The Autoimmune Paleo Cookbook: An Allergen-Free Approach to Managing Chronic Illness.* Trescott LLC, 2014.

FERMENTATION COOKBOOKS

Christensen, Emma. *True Brews: How to Craft Fermented Cider, Beer, Wine, Sake, Soda, Mead, Kefir, and Kombucha at Home.* Berkeley, CA: Ten Speed Press, 2013.

Katz, Sandor Ellix. *The Art of Fermentation: An In-Depth Exploration of Essential Concepts and Processes from Around the World.* White River Junction, VT: Chelsea Green Publishing, 2012.

Lewin, Alex. *Real Food Fermentation: Preserving Whole Fresh Food with Live Cultures in Your Home Kitchen.* Beverly, MA: Quarry Books, 2012.

REFERENCES FOR "FINDING PALEO" AND "THE WHY, WHAT, AND HOW OF PALEO"

Ballantyne, Sarah. *The Paleo Approach: Reverse Autoimmune Disease and Heal Your Body.* Las Vegas: Victory Belt Publishing, 2013. 90, 214.

Durant, John. *The Paleo Manifesto: Ancient Wisdom for Lifelong Health.* New York: Harmony Books, 2013. 16.

Fasano, Alessio. *Gluten Freedom.* New York: Wiley General Trade, 2014. 5, 24, 25.

Monterey Bay Aquarium Seafood Watch. "Fishing and Farming Methods." www.seafoodwatch.org/ocean-issues/fishing-and-farming-methods.

Sisson, Mark. "Mystery Meat: Imitation Crab." *Mark's Daily Apple.* March 12, 2008. www.marksdailyapple.com/imitation-crab/#axzz3HyQtP6ii.

Wolf, Robb. *The Paleo Solution: The Original Human Diet.* Las Vegas: Victory Belt Publishing, 2010. Kindle edition. 89.

Recipe Index

BASICS

56 Ghee

58 Dairy-Free Creamy Caesar Dressing

60 Maple Balsamic Salad Dressing

62 Spicy Citrus Salad Dressing

64 Homemade Aioli

66 Smoky Chipotle Aioli

66 Extra-Garlicky Sriracha Aioli

68 Salsa

70 Apple Butter

72 Apple Butter BBQ Sauce

74 Smoky Pineapple BBQ Sauce

76 Bone Broth

78 Basic Cupcake Icing

80 Chocolate Sauce

82 Caramel Sauce

84 Coconut Flour Bar Base

FERMENTED FOODS & DRINKS

90 Raw Sauerkraut

92 Rainbow Sauerkraut

94 Fermented Jalapeño Peppers

96 Fermented Sriracha Sauce

98 Garlic Dill Pickles

DITCH THE WHEAT

100

Kombucha

102

Watermelon Kiwi Kombucha

104

Strawberry Basil Kombucha

106

Berry Ginger Kombucha

108

Ginger Bug

110

Cherry Ginger Soda

112

Coconut Milk Yogurt

CRACKERS, WRAPS, BREADS, BAGELS & MUFFINS

116

Vegetable Crackers

118

"Whole-Grain" Crackers

120

"Everything Bagel"–Inspired Crackers

122

Banana Muffins

124

Fruit Jam Muffins

126

Morning Glory Muffins

128

Paleo Bread

130

Grain-Free Tortillas

132

Sandwich Buns

134

Grain-Free Bagels

136

Sweet Potato Drop Biscuits

BREAKFAST FAVORITES

140
Maple Sage
Breakfast Sausages

142
Pizza
Breakfast Sausages

144
The Original DTW
Meat Bagel

146
Meat French Toast

148
Baked Eggs

150
On-the-Go Eggs

152
Spicy Brunch Casserole

154
Grain-Free Waffles

156
Coconut Flour Pancakes

158
Yuca Hash Browns

SNACKS & STARTERS

162
Sweet Potato Nacho Dip

164
Apple Butter
Chicken Liver Pâté

166
Dates Stuffed with
Coconut Butter

168
Plantain Chips

170
BBQ Kale Chips

172
Spicy Nori Chips

174
Artichoke with
Bacon Spinach Dip

176
Sun-Dried Tomato &
Basil Hummus

178
Onion Fries

180
Salted Mexican
Chocolate Clusters

SOUPS & SALADS

184
Hearty Beef Stew

186
Dairy-Free
Shrimp Bisque

188
Roasted Butternut
Squash Soup

190
Roasted Garlic &
Sweet Red Pepper Soup

192
Roasted Tomato &
Basil Soup

194

Chicken Enchilada Soup

196

Tomato Basil Salad

198

BLT Wedge Salad

200

Kale Citrus Salad

202

Apple Walnut Salad

204

Warm Dandelion
Pear Salad

MAIN MEALS

208

Salmon with
Mango Salsa

210

Curry Shrimp Dish

212

Spicy Fish Cakes with
Dipping Sauce

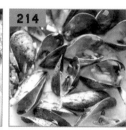

214

Mussels with
Butter Broth

216

Dijon & Herb Almond-
Crusted Snapper

218

Spicy Vietnamese
Rainbow Trout

220

Ginger Beef Stir-Fry

222

Smoky Chipotle Aioli
Burgers with
Crunchy Mango Slaw

224

Thyme Dijon Mustard
Prime Rib

226

Meatloaf with
Maple Balsamic Glaze

228

Swedish Meatballs

230

Beef Tongue Tacos

232

Chicken Fingers with
Dipping Sauce

234

Cilantro Maple Sriracha
Chicken Wings

236

Lemon Rosemary
Roast Chicken

238
Dairy-Free
Butter Chicken

240
Honey Mustard Garlic
Chicken Thighs

242
Hungarian
Cabbage Rolls

246
Smoky Pineapple
Pulled Pork

248
Apple Butter
BBQ Ribs

250
Spinach, Raisin &
Pine Nut–Stuffed
Pork Loin

252
Thyme Mushroom
Pork Chops

254
Creamy Tomato
Mushroom
Chicken Pasta

256
Mango Prosciutto
Grain-Free Pizza

258
Grain-Free Lasagna

SIDES

262
Roasted Cauliflower

264
Loaded Mashed
Cauliflower with
Bacon & Green Onions

266
Prosciutto-Wrapped
Asparagus

268
Savory Pureed
Butternut Squash

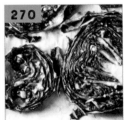
270
Garlic-Roasted Cabbage

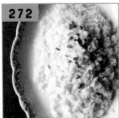
272
Cauliflower Rice

274
Oven-Baked
Sweet Potato Fries

276
Herb-Roasted
Fingerling Potatoes

278
Crispy Sautéed Kale
with Bacon & Onions

280
Mashed Banana
Sweet Potatoes

282
Roasted Carrots
with a Kick

284
Roasted Leeks

DESSERTS

288
Birthday Cake

290
Chocolate Cake

292
Carrot Cake
Cupcakes

294
Caramel Chocolate
Nut Bars

296
Brownies

298
Cinnamon Buns

300
Apple Crumble

302
Chocolate-Dipped
Honeycomb

304
Dad's N'Oatmeal
Cookies

306
Chocolate Chip Cookies

308
Strawberry Swirl
Ice Cream

310
Chocolate Truffle
Custard with
Salted Cashew Crust

Allergen Index

Recipe	Page	Egg-Free	Dairy-Free	Nut-Free
Ghee	56	●	●	●
Dairy-Free Creamy Caesar Dressing	58		●	●
Maple Balsamic Salad Dressing	60	●	●	●
Spicy Citrus Salad Dressing	62	●	●	●
Homemade Aioli	64		●	●
Smoky Chipotle Aioli	66		●	●
Extra-Garlicky Sriracha Aioli	66		●	●
Salsa	68	●	●	●
Apple Butter	70	●	●	●
Apple Butter BBQ Sauce	72	●	●	●
Smoky Pineapple BBQ Sauce	74	●	●	●
Bone Broth	76	●	●	●
Basic Cupcake Icing	78	●	●	●
Chocolate Sauce	80	●	●	
Caramel Sauce	82	●	●	●
Coconut Flour Bar Base	84		●	●
Raw Sauerkraut	90	●	●	●
Rainbow Sauerkraut	92	●	●	●
Fermented Jalapeño Peppers	94	●	●	●
Fermented Sriracha Sauce	96	●	●	●
Garlic Dill Pickles	98	●	●	●
Kombucha	100	●	●	●
Watermelon Kiwi Kombucha	102	●	●	●
Strawberry Basil Kombucha	104	●	●	●
Berry Ginger Kombucha	106	●	●	●
Ginger Bug	108	●	●	●
Cherry Ginger Soda	110	●	●	●
Coconut Milk Yogurt	112	●	●	●
Vegetable Crackers	116	●	●	●
"Whole-Grain" Crackers	118	●	●	●
"Everything Bagel"–Inspired Crackers	120	●	●	●
Banana Muffins	122		●	●
Fruit Jam Muffins	124		●	●
Morning Glory Muffins	126		●	●
Paleo Bread	128		●	
Grain-Free Tortillas	130	●	●	
Sandwich Buns	132		●	
Grain-Free Bagels	134		●	
Sweet Potato Drop Biscuits	136			●
Maple Sage Breakfast Sausages	140	●	●	●
Pizza Breakfast Sausages	142	●	●	●
The Original DTW Meat Bagel	144		●	●
Meat French Toast	146		●	●
Baked Eggs	148		●	●
On-the-Go Eggs	150		●	●
Spicy Brunch Casserole	152		●	●
Grain-Free Waffles	154		●	
Coconut Flour Pancakes	156		●	●
Yuca Hash Browns	158	●	●	●
Sweet Potato Nacho Dip	162	●	●	●
Apple Butter Chicken Liver Pâté	164	●		●
Dates Stuffed with Coconut Butter	166	●	●	●
Plantain Chips	168	●	●	●
BBQ Kale Chips	170	●	●	●
Spicy Nori Chips	172	●	●	●
Artichoke with Bacon Spinach Dip	174		●	●
Sun-Dried Tomato & Basil Hummus	176	●	●	●
Onion Fries	178		●	●
Salted Mexican Chocolate Clusters	180	●	●	

Recipe	Page	Egg-Free	Dairy-Free	Nut-Free
Hearty Beef Stew	184	●	●	●
Dairy-Free Shrimp Bisque	186	●	●	●
Roasted Butternut Squash Soup	188	●	●	●
Roasted Garlic & Sweet Red Pepper Soup	190	●	●	●
Roasted Tomato & Basil Soup	192	●	●	●
Chicken Enchilada Soup	194	●	●	●
Tomato Basil Salad	196	●	●	●
BLT Wedge Salad	198		●	●
Kale Citrus Salad	200	●	●	
Apple Walnut Salad	202	●	●	
Warm Dandelion Pear Salad	204	●	●	●
Salmon with Mango Salsa	208	●	●	●
Curry Shrimp Dish	210	●	●	
Spicy Fish Cakes with Dipping Sauce	212		●	
Mussels with Butter Broth	214	●		●
Dijon & Herb Almond-Crusted Snapper	216	●	●	
Spicy Vietnamese Rainbow Trout	218	●	●	●
Ginger Beef Stir-Fry	220	●	●	●
Smoky Chipotle Aioli Burgers with Crunchy Mango Slaw	222		●	●
Thyme Dijon Mustard Prime Rib	224	●	●	●
Meatloaf with Maple Balsamic Glaze	226		●	●
Swedish Meatballs	228		●	●
Beef Tongue Tacos	230	●	●	
Chicken Fingers with Dipping Sauce	232		●	
Cilantro Maple Sriracha Chicken Wings	234	●	●	●
Lemon Rosemary Roast Chicken	236	●	●	●
Dairy-Free Butter Chicken	238	●	●	●
Honey Mustard Garlic Chicken Thighs	240	●	●	●
Hungarian Cabbage Rolls	242	●	●	●
Smoky Pineapple Pulled Pork	246	●	●	●
Apple Butter BBQ Ribs	248	●	●	●
Spinach, Raisin & Pine Nut–Stuffed Pork Loin	250	●	●	
Thyme Mushroom Pork Chops	252	●		
Creamy Tomato Mushroom Chicken Pasta	254	●	●	●
Mango Prosciutto Grain-Free Pizza	256		●	●
Grain-Free Lasagna	258	●	●	
Roasted Cauliflower	262	●	●	●
Loaded Mashed Cauliflower with Bacon & Green Onions	264	●	●	●
Prosciutto-Wrapped Asparagus	266	●	●	●
Savory Pureed Butternut Squash	268	●	●	●
Garlic-Roasted Cabbage	270	●	●	●
Cauliflower Rice	272	●	●	●
Oven-Baked Sweet Potato Fries	274	●	●	●
Herb-Roasted Fingerling Potatoes	276	●	●	●
Crispy Sautéed Kale with Bacon & Onions	278	●	●	●
Mashed Banana Sweet Potatoes	280	●		●
Roasted Carrots with a Kick	282	●	●	●
Roasted Leeks	284	●	●	●
Birthday Cake	288		●	●
Chocolate Cake	290		●	●
Carrot Cake Cupcakes	292		●	
Caramel Chocolate Nut Bars	294		●	
Brownies	296		●	
Cinnamon Buns	298		●	
Apple Crumble	300	●	●	
Chocolate-Dipped Honeycomb	302	●	●	●
Dad's N'Oatmeal Cookies	304		●	
Chocolate Chip Cookies	306		●	
Strawberry Swirl Ice Cream	308		●	●
Chocolate Truffle Custard with Salted Cashew Crust	310		●	

General Index

DITCH THE WHEAT